P9-DUZ-863

PS PÚ2 .05J

WESTERN VIEWS AND EASTERN VISIONS

Eugene Ostroff
Curator of Photography
National Museum of American History
Smithsonian Institution

Published by the
Smithsonian Institution Traveling
Exhibition Service
with the cooperation of the
United States Geological Survey
1981

WITHDRAWN

© 1981 by Smithsonian Institution
All rights reserved.

Library of Congress Cataloging in
Publication Data

Ostroff, Eugene.
Western views and Eastern visions.

Prepared in conjunction with an
exhibition presented by the
Smithsonian Institution Traveling
Exhibition Service.
Bibliography: p. 116
1. Photography—The West—History
—Exhibitions. I. Smithsonian Institu-
tion. Traveling Exhibition Service.
II. Title.
TR23.6.087   779'.9978   81-70
ISBN 0-86528-005-3

International Standard Book
Number: 0-86528-005-3

SITES is a program activity of the
Smithsonian Institution that organizes
and circulates exhibitions on art,
history, and science to institutions in
the United States and abroad.

Designed by Invisions, Ltd.,
Washington, D.C.
Composed in Baskerline by Harlowe
Typography, Inc.
Printed on Sonata Natural Vellum
and Lustro Offset Enamel by Eastern
Press, New Haven, Connecticut

Illustrated on cover:

"North from Berthoud Pass"
Photograph by William Henry
Jackson, 1874, see page 58, figure 36.

For sale by the Superintendent of
Documents
United States Government Printing Office
Washington, D.C. 20402
Price: $11.00
Stock Number 047-000-0037-7

CONTENTS

FOREWORD

Western Views and Eastern Visions draws on significant work of photographers and artists of the middle and late nineteenth century during the westward movement—work that is important not only for its intrinsic interest and artistic merit but in particular for its relationship to the scientific surveys for which much of it was done and to the rapid technological improvements in photography of the period that paralleled the country's own coming of age. It is most appropriate that this exhibition and book be presented by the Smithsonian Insitution as it combines material culture—photography, art, science and technology—with history and geography to offer a glimpse at an exciting period in the history of this country.

In presenting this exhibition, the Smithsonian Insitution Traveling Exhibition Service is indebted to Eugene Ostroff, Curator of Photography at the National Museum of American History, for his expertise and organization, and to the U.S. Geological Survey for its financial and research support. The USGS was also among the many federal and municipal lenders to the exhibition. It is not unusual for SITES to be the recipient of such good will and cooperation. Almost every one of SITES' 150 exhibitions currently traveling in the United States and abroad was produced with a similar combination.

A traveling exhibition of this size and scope requires expert supervision. As usual, the many members of SITES' staff assigned to this project performed admirably. Deserving special note is Exhibition Coordinator Deborah Dawson. Others to be thanked include Registrar Emily Dyer and Publications Officer Andrea Stevens.

Peggy A. Loar
Director, SITES

ACKNOWLEDGEMENTS

This exhibition and catalog became a reality through the cooperation of numerous people who generously provided their expertise. At the Smithsonian Institution, I would like to thank the following people and departments: Smithsonian Institution Traveling Exhibition Service: Dennis Gould (former Director), Deborah Dawson and Andrea Stevens; Division of Photographic History: Linda Benbow, Harry Patton and volunteers Jacqueline Buell and Kurt Maier; Collections Management Department: Thomas Bush, Linda Cook, James Lee, Martha Morris, Charles Rowell and John Ryan; Photographic Services: Alfred Harrell, Mary Ellen McCaffrey, Llewellyn Thomas and Jeffrey Tinsley; Office of Exhibits: Assistant Director, Exhibits Benjamin Lawless, and Barbara J. Allen, Robert Conklin, Anthony Di Stefano, Helen S. Holman, John H. Houser, Andrew A. Kolarik, Walter N. Lewis, John E. Lynch, Sr., Albert P. Martin, Nicholas Michnya, John Ondish, Hubert J. Ray, volunteers Lisa Duennebrier, Karen Jennifer, Janna Leepson and Kathryn Mayer; Rare Book Conservation Laboratory: Johannes Hyltoft and staff. The exhibition was designed by Nadya Makovenyi.

I would also like to thank the staffs of other organizations who gave invaluable assistance by loaning and identifying items in the exhibition: United States Department of the Interior: Robert Mendelsohn, Assistant to the Secretary; National Park Service: Priscilla Baker and Marc Sagan; United States Geological Survey for the identification of all photographs and some of the artwork; Yellowstone National Park, Yosemite National Park and Grand Teton National Park; National Archives and Records Service, Library of Congress, Colorado Historical Society and the Denver Public Library. For their rapid response and assistance with the exhibition, I am grateful to the National Geographic Society: David Chisman, Ronald Langendorfer, Carl Shrader and Alfred Yee.

I would like to express special appreciation to David Haberstich, Smithsonian's Division of Photographic History, for his wholehearted cooperation on both the exhibition and catalog projects.   — E.O.

THE WEST COMES EAST

When President Thomas Jefferson signed the Louisiana Purchase in 1803, the territory of the United States doubled. With this addition of 828,000 square miles the nation's western boundary was moved from the Mississippi River to the Rocky Mountains. The newly acquired region west of the Mississippi was of enormous interest both to government officials and the public, but few trained observers had ever seen this vast region and, therefore, available information was scant and often unreliable.

To begin exploring at least a part of this area and find a route from the Mississippi to the Pacific, President Jefferson sent Captains Meriwether Lewis and William Clark on a cross-continental expedition in 1804-1806. When their remarkable report was published after their return, public and governmental interest in the West increased dramatically. The Federal government, California, commercial firms, and even foreign royalty sponsored subsequent expeditions. The common goal was to map the land and inventory its resources. These projects produced maps and scientific descriptions as well as samples from the field for study and classification.

Executive, legislative and public interest was aroused by the accounts of these expeditions. However, some of the very wonders and grandeurs described by the explorers taxed the credulity of readers.

To a high percentage of the general public there was far more at stake than an idle, or even scientific curiosity about the new region. The United States experienced five severe depressions during the nineteenth century. Unemployment was high, and the thousands of immigrants who poured into the country each year aggravated the economic situation. Bank failures were widespread and paper money was often in disrepute. To many Americans—native and newly arrived—the promise of rich resources and bargain land of the West seemed an easy way out of their difficulties. In the following decades thousands of emigrants were to move across the continent in search of a better life.

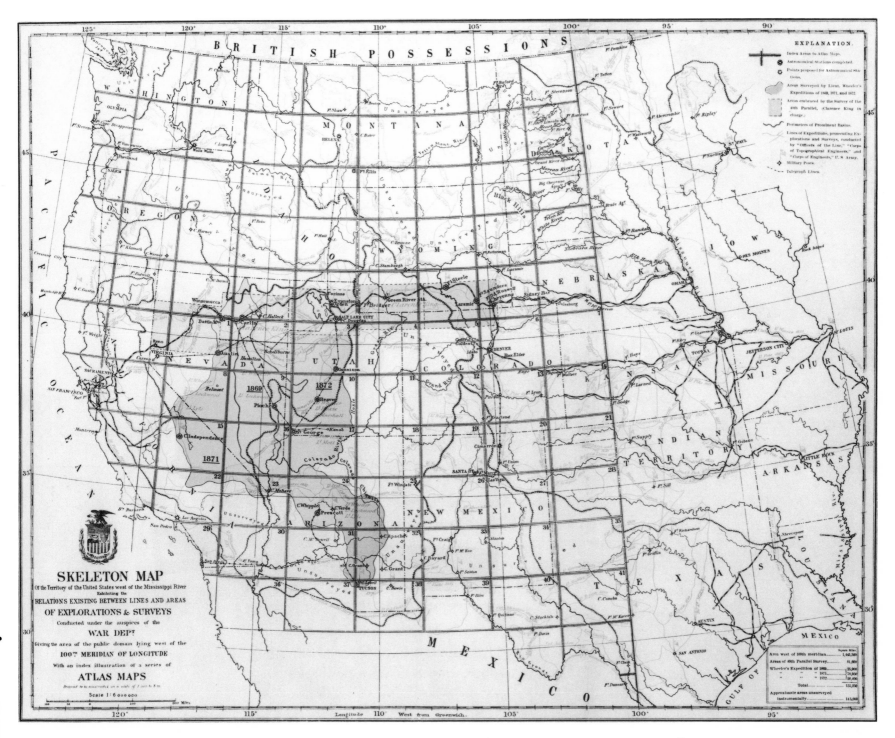

SKELETON MAP
Of the Territory of the United States west of the Mississippi River
Exhibiting the
RELATIONS EXISTING BETWEEN LINES AND AREAS
OF EXPLORATIONS & SURVEYS
Conducted under the auspices of the
WAR DEP.T
Giving the area of the public domain lying west of the
100.TH MERIDIAN OF LONGITUDE
With an index illustration of a series of
ATLAS MAPS

Scale 1:6000000

There was some hard evidence to support the dream. Fur trappers and trading companies who became wealthy in the West were living proof that the land did offer great riches. The very fact that men survived and prospered in the wilderness demonstrated that the land was not completely inhospitable. Yet uprooting a family from the known—unfavorable as it might be—for a hazardous journey into the unknown was not a light undertaking. Therefore, the demand for additional, accurate information about the West—information one could rely on—mounted steadily.

Early Visual Documentation

The largest and most useful flow of information about the unexplored West came from government-sponsored expeditions and railroad surveys. Major Stephen H. Long, Topographical Bureau, and other expedition leaders, recognized the need to provide fuller and more meaningful visual documentation of their explorations. Long decided to supplement his written report with illustrations of his especially notable findings. When he set out on his 1819-20 expedition to the Rockies, he took along Samuel Seymour, probably the first staff artist to accompany a western expedition. In his proposal, Long wrote:

Mr. Seymour, as painter for the expedition, will furnish sketches of landscapes, whenever we meet with any distinguished for their beauty and grandeur. He will also paint miniature likenesses, or portraits if required, of distinguished Indians, and exhibit groups of savages engaged in celebrating their festivals, or sitting in council, and in general illustrate any subject, that may be deemed appropriate in his art.

Assistant naturalist Titian Ramsey Peale had the responsibility of "sketching the stratification of rocks, earths, etc. as presented on the declivities of precipices."[1]

At the end of the expedition, Long reported that Seymour's landscape views "are one hundred and fifty in number; of these sixty have been finished," and "The sketches ... by Mr. Peale amount to one hundred and twenty-two; of these twenty-one only were finished, the residue being merely outlines of quadrapeds, birds, insects, etc."[2] Long included the work of both men in his official report and some of the art was displayed to the public in a museum exhibit.

Major Long's example was soon followed by other explorers. When Prince Maximilian of Weid-Neuwied, a dedicated Prussian naturalist, made the long trip from Europe to pursue an expedition to the West in 1833, he took along Karl Bodmer, the Swiss artist, to observe and record Indian life and the flora and fauna of the area. By the 1850s, painters and illustrators were accepted as important adjuncts to western explorations. However, most of the early art work illustrating the West was seen by a limited audience. Some appeared in scientific and popular publications as lithographs,

Detail of untitled pencil and chalk drawing by Thomas A. Ayres, 1855, see page 52, figure 24.

engravings, and woodcuts; others were exhibited as originals. Compared to the public exposure to the media in our times, however, the total circulation of this early material was rather limited.

Techniques for reproducing and printing illustrative material were slow and done largely by hand; inexpensive, mass-produced systems of photomechanical printing did not appear until the end of the century. After returning from expeditions, artists used their sketches, watercolors, and usually, some imagination to create their more elaborate work.

Artistic license, however, was not always well received. When a large painting of the West by Albert Bierstadt was displayed at the National Academy of Design, the work was attacked in 1867 as being "wholly untrue and inartistic. . . . This last picture of Mr. Bierstadt's [The Domes of Yo Semite] seems to be better than any he has shown us before. . . . [However] the rocks are not rocks . . . the water does not fall in a way . . . [similar to] real water."[3]

Speaking through one of his characters in his book, *Mountaineering in the Sierra Nevada*, Clarence King, a writer-explorer, expressed one contemporary criticism of Bierstadt's Western art:

It's all Bierstadt and Bierstadt and Bierstadt nowadays! What has he done but twist and skew and distort and discolor and belittle and be-pretty this whole doggonned country? Why, his mountains are too high and too slim; they'd blow over in one of our fall winds.

I've . . . [spent] two summers in Yosemite, and honest now, when I stood right up in front of his picture, I didn't know it.[4]

Such barbs—which were not by any means directed only at Bierstadt's work—brought the documentary accuracy of all Western art into question. Nevertheless, this did not lead to a widespread dismissal of all Western paintings and drawings as nothing more than the products of romantic artists, or of the written reports of the area as highly fictional. Rather, it furthered a national concern for some kind of incontrovertible proof to substantiate the existence of the wonders described and portrayed by explorers and artists. That kind of proof could be provided only by photography. Actually, even the word "photography" did not yet exist when Lewis and Clark left on their expedition in 1804. Not until thirty-five years later did Louis Jacques Mandé Daguerre invent the first practical photographic process, the daguerreotype.

The Daguerreotype

Even after the daguerreotype won worldwide acclaim there were reasons why it was not widely used for expeditionary purposes in the West. This was not only because the pictures were difficult to make—extreme care and expertise were needed to prepare and process plates—but largely because the final image could be seen only by a limited audience. The fragile image rested delicately on the silver-plated surface of a copper sheet that needed careful handling because even an accidental brush of a finger removed the image forever. To protect the pictures each plate was permanently mounted behind glass in its own small case, a cumbersome arrangement that made viewing the pictures awkward. Furthermore, each image was unique and could not be duplicated except by rephotographing the original, a practice not frequently followed. Therefore only a relatively few people ever saw the results, unless the images were produced as woodcuts or engravings.

Despite their awareness of the disadvantages of daguerreotype, the leaders of several antebellum expeditions encouraged the use of this process. In 1853 artist/photographer John Mix Stanley made daguerreotypes of Indians while accompanying the Isaac I. Stevens survey of a northen railroad route to the Pacific.[5] Col. John Charles Frémont foresaw the importance of such documentary work. In 1853 he invited thirty-eight-year-old artist/daguerreotypist Solomon Nuñes Carvalho to join his party in an "Exploring Expedition across the Rocky Mountains."[6] Despite temperatures which dropped to 20° or 30°(F) below zero and near-starvation conditions, Carvalho successfully made daguerreotypes and brought them back to be copied at the Brady studio in New York. These images, along with sketches by Carvalho, were used in 1855-56 as studies for oil paintings by the artist James Hamilton, and for wood engravings and sketches by other artists.[7]

The activities of adventurer-daguerreotypist J. Wesley Jones, one of the more successful photographic pioneers, were dramatically described in 1854 by John Ross Dix.[8] To traverse the West in 1851, Jones fitted out a daguerreotype carriage and brought together a corps of sketching artists including William Quesenberg, editor of the Sacramento Union; William Shew of Boston; Jacob Shew of Baltimore; and S. L. Shaw of New Orleans ". . . a total of twenty . . . with a cavalcade of fifty mules."[9]

Jones was described as "fighting his way stubbornly through

Indian territory—daguerreotyping every point of the way, gun in hand," while making photographs in California, Nebraska, and Utah. About 200 miles from the Great Salt Lake, he was menaced by an Indian war party which:

advanced with lances poised, ready for battle ... [the photographer] ... turned upon them his camera ... held his lighted cigar ... [close] to the instrument. These savages had heard strange stories of thunder on wheels, which had, in one terrific burst, swept away whole parties of red skins. Panic-stricken they paused ... veered to the right ... but the strange mortar followed them. ... Pop, pop, pop! went a revolver from beneath the instrument. ... They could no longer stand it; but with a simultaneous yell, broke away towards the rocks. ...

Forever after this incident was called "Jones' charge upon the Indians with the daguerreotype instrument."[10] Jones later used sketches and 1,500 daguerreotypes of the Rocky Mountains and Sierra Nevadas, the deserts, the plains, and the Great Salt Lake area to produce a gigantic panoramic painting, called the Great Pantoscope which was displayed in Boston and New York.

Wet-Plate Photography: A Major Breakthrough

About the time the daguerreotype process was announced in 1839, another system, the photogenic drawing, was introduced by William Henry Fox Talbot of England. By 1841 Talbot introduced the process called the calotype that revolutionized the entire approach to photography. Talbot established the method of using a negative to produce unlimited numbers of prints. Unfortunately, the calotype negative used a sheet of paper as a support, and the fibrous, translucent characteristics of the paper diffused the light passing through the negative thereby softening the image definition and extending printing time. Technical problems with the paper sheet itself in this process were never fully solved and the results were often unpredictable. There was another handicap; the calotype took longer to expose than the daguerreotype.

The glass plate negative of the collodion process, introduced in 1851, provided the technical breakthrough that was needed: a new, chemically inert transparent support. A limitless number of prints could be made from the plate without the "softer" image quality of the calotype, and the required exposure time was less, both for taking pictures and making prints.

Immediately before taking each picture, the photographer manufactured the light-sensitive coating on the glass plate surface. Exposures were made while the coating was damp, i.e., during the time of maximum sensitivity. The plate was processed immediately so that solutions penetrated the still-soft collodion. Therefore, a darkroom was needed close to the camera. Although these restrictions severely slowed down picture-taking, they offered a fringe benefit—the

"Robinson's Landing, Mouth of Colorado River," detail of monochrome lithograph from a drawing by J.J. Young based on a wet-plate photograph by 1st Lt. Joseph Christmas Ives, 1857, see page 26, figure 1.

results were known immediately. If the image was faulty, the picture could be redone.

Despite the advantages offered by the collodion process, outdoor photography remained a cumbersome, laborious technique that presented severe problems away from a studio darkroom. These difficulties caused the nearby complete failure of collodion plates when first used on western expeditions. For example, Lt. Joseph Ives used a wet-plate photographic outfit to make his own pictures along the Colorado River in 1858. Very likely he wanted to satisfy his own curiosity about this new image-making medium and test its effectiveness for expeditionary purposes. Despite several attempts at taking pictures around the camp and nearby river, his results were only partially successful. Although Ives attributed the poor results to deteriorated chemicals, glaring light, and image movement caused by hot air rising from the ground, it probably was his inexperience with the process that led to his failure. His difficulties were resolved early in the trip when strong winds hit the camp and destroyed "the photographic tent [and] made a clean thing of it, apparatus and all." Relieved of this burden, Ives stated that this loss was of "comparatively little importance."[11] Despite his complete lack of enthusiasm about using photography for field work, one of his photographs was used as the basis for an illustration in the final report (see Fig. 1).

Expeditionary photography received a decisive boost in the summer of 1859, when Albert Bierstadt brought photographer S. F. Frost of Boston with a "full corps of artists" (at their own expense) on F. W. Lander's survey of a wagon route to the Rockies. Bierstadt had begun using photographs for reference purposes at his studio when doing his paintings. Lander, who served as superintendent of wagon routes at Ft. Kearny, Nebraska, for the Department of the Interior, was so deeply impressed with the photography and art work done by the group that he reported:

They have taken sketches of the most remarkable of the views along the

"Tufa Mounds, Pyramid Lake, Nevada," detail of photograph by Timothy H. O'Sullivan, probably 1867, see page 90, figure 86A.

route, and a set of stereoscopic views of emigrant trains, Indians, camp scenes, etc., which are highly valuable and would be interesting to the country.[12]

Expanded Use

The public learned more about the value of using photographs on expeditions through the lead article of the September 1869 issue of *Harper's New Monthly Magazine.* This story, "Photographs from the High Rockies," carried thirteen wood engravings copied from photographs taken on Clarence King's survey (the U.S. Geological Exploration of the Fortieth Parallel) during 1867-68; the text was probably based on information supplied by Timothy H. O'Sullivan, the expedition's photographer.[13]

Another strong advocate of photography was Ferdinand Vandeveer Hayden who led a second Federal survey of territories in the West and was also impressed with the outstanding advantages of photographic documentation and publicity. In 1870 he wrote in his book *Sun Pictures of Rocky Mountain Scenery,* which included thirty photographs by A. J. Russell, that photographs provided "the nearest approach to a truthful delineation of nature."[14] Hayden stated that J.D. Whitney's *The Yosemite Book* (1868), containing photographs by Carleton Watkins, had inspired his own volume.[15] In *Sun Pictures,* Hayden used photographs for scientific purposes stating:

The increasing interest now taken in the science of geology, has led me to believe that a volume embodying the principal geological facts . . . would be read with interest. The photographs I have selected . . . illustrate the peculiar surface features, given to the country by geological formation . . . weathering peculiar to the granites of the first range of mountains . . . the Triassic sandstones . . .[16]

By 1870, photography approached full acceptance for use on expeditions. Expedition leaders and potential sponsors recognized that photographs could highlight descriptions in their final reports. They added another dimension to the impact of the written word. These images were relied upon to support evidence of sights seen in

"Ridge of Archaean Quartzite—Humboldt Range," detail of toned photolithograph by Julius Bien, 1877, see page 109, figure 114B.

the field. Lithographs, probably photolithographs, containing considerable handwork,[17] copied from photographs appeared more often in government survey reports. In spite of the progress made by photography, it did not replace specialized drawings done in the field by artists such as William Henry Holmes. These views of geological and topographical features subtly emphasized the scientific details of landscapes in a unique style which could not be matched by the photographic techniques of the times.

Photographer William Henry Jackson later emphasized that even after the findings of General Henry D. Washburn and Nathaniel P. Langford's 1870 Yellowstone expedition had been published:[18]

the doubting Thomases demanded still further proof . . . it was Hayden . . . who determined to satisfy them. If taxpayers and Congressmen alike wanted more evidence, none of them wanted it half so much as Dr. Hayden . . . [he] saw how a widespread public interest could keep his survey alive permanently. Hayden knew that Congress would keep on with its annual appropriations exactly as long as the people were ready to foot the bill, and he was determined to make them keep wanting to. That was where I came in. No photographs had as yet been published, *and Dr. Hayden was determined that the first ones should be good. A series of fine pictures would not only supplement his final report but tell the story to thousands who might never read it . . . but an astonishing number of people bought finished photographs to hang on their walls, or to view through stereoscopes.*[19]

Jackson described "the popularization of the work of the survey by means of photographs. Great efforts were made each year therefore, to come back with something of more than ordinary interest, something new and unique that had never been photographed before. Nearly every trip we had something of this kind to lay before official Washington."[20]

Another strong proponent of photography, Lt. George Montague Wheeler (who led a third western survey for the Corps of Engineers) emphasized his belief in the broader role of photography by stating in the manuscript for the 1872 report on his U.S. Surveys West of the

EXPEDITION OF 1873.

1st Lieut. GEO M WHEELER,
Corps of Engineers Commanding.

"**Old Pueblo Ruins, Cañon de Chelle, N.M.,**"
stereograph by Timothy H. O'Sullivan,
1873, see page 31, figure 7A.

100th Meridian that the "professional uses of photography beyond recording scenic features were few." He was dissatisfied that material data gathered from its use "apply only to . . . geology, and natural history." Wheeler was confident that the full potential of photography had not yet been realized and that with "skilled labor, and the refinement of instruments [he might be able to] give value to the horizontal, and vertical measurements, upon a photographic picture." These measurements then could be used for comparison purposes to note any changes that might occur in the future. Photography also would be of assistance "in the publication of maps and illustrations." Wheeler urged the War Department to incorporate photography as a permanent part of surveys and encouraged them to establish a photographic corps consisting of several photographers who could be assigned to expeditions.[21]

In reviewing the preparations and procedures used by western expeditionary photographers, it becomes apparent that, in addition to technical skills, cameramen needed talent, infinite patience, full dedication—and a strong back. The plates, equipment, and other supplies were heavy and fragile. The technical demands of the process required materials of great volume and weight when this work was done in the field.

Equipment

When photographing in the field in the 1870s, the camera was set in place, and the scene composed and focused in the camera. The light-sensitive coating was made in the portable darkroom by pouring a chemically treated, honey-thick, collodion solution onto the plate. The solution was uniformly distributed across its surface by tilting and rotating it, and any excess was poured back into a container. A brief dip in a chemical mix produced the needed light sensitivity. The plate was then inserted in a light-tight holder, similar in construction to sheet-film holders used by photographers today. The holder was placed in the camera and the exposure made. The plate was developed and fixed, in the portable darkroom,

Detail of untitled photograph by Timothy H. O'Sullivan shows his wagon and photographic unit, 1867, see page 112, figure 117.

usually a light-proof tent on expeditions. Washing was usually done outside the tent. This entire procedure was repeated for each picture. Human subjects had to wait while these time-consuming steps were carried out, so pictures were almost never unposed, informal "snapshots." Skittish animal life or anything in fast motion eluded the photographic plate.

Exposure times varied considerably, depending upon variation in sensitivity among chemical-coating mixtures; subject matter (dark or light, and its color), and daylight conditions (time of day, year, weather). One landscape photographer reported in 1869 that minimum exposures could vary between five seconds and three minutes.[22] For particularly poor conditions, exposures could always be extended. Jackson reported that his exposures varied from "instantaneous [approximately 1/10 second] . . . with a primitive drop shutter, to 10 to 15 seconds on a clear day."[23]

Expeditionary photography was physically arduous due to the variety and volume of equipment and the chemicals and supplies needed for doing a season's work in the field away from sources of supply. Glass plates, bottles for chemicals, and other necessities, were not only extraordinarily heavy and awkward to carry over rough terrain but required care and protective packing to prevent breakage. As enlargers were not yet widely used, glass plate negatives were the same size as the final prints; 11 x 14-inch prints required 11 x 14-inch glass for the negatives. In addition, usually at least two cameras were used in the field, one for regular format photography and the other for stereo work, which required a twin lens camera plus a tripod and darkroom tent.

Clarence King discussed equipment needs for a forthcoming expedition with photographer O'Sullivan and then asked Maj. General Andrew A. Humphreys, Chief of Engineers, on April 22, 1867, to approve this "memorandum of Photographic Instruments and Materials Required for Geological Exploration of the 40th Parallel,"[24]

One Camera-Box for 9 x 12 plates
One Tripod Stand for same
Camera for Stereoscopic views
One Tube for 9 x 12 views, by Zentmeyer of Phila.
One Pair of globe tubes for stereoscopes
75 English Patent Plates 9 x 12 in boxes of 25
50 English Patent Plates 8 x 10 in boxes of 25
1 Extra plate box to contain 25 plates for each size, vs 9 x 12 and 8 x 10
1 Hard Rubber bath for 9 x 12 plates with 2 dippers
Two Hydrometers for silver solutions
1 Eight ounce fluid measuring glass
1 Glass filter and 2 packages of 13 in. filter paper
1 small photographic tent
1 Plate holder for cleaning plates of 9 x 12 in.
1 Plate holder for cleaning plates of 8 x 10 in.
6 pounds nitrate of silver
3 pounds rotten stone finely powdered
6 oz. Iodide of Potassium
3 oz. Iodide of Cadmium
3 ounces Bromide of Ammonium
3 ounces Bromide of Cadmium
6 oz. Crystalized Iodine
5 Pounds Cyanide of Potassium
4 Pounds Negative Varnish
1 Black cloth for focus shade

Problems of Photography

Jackson described how such equipment was employed in the field. If suitable trails ran reasonably close to photographic sites, a horse-drawn darkroom-wagon might be used. More remote regions required pack-mules or horses to transport gear to sites. In areas that defied passage by animals, supplies were back-packed by the photographer. Jackson reported:

outfitting for a season's work was a big and serious undertaking . . . enlarging methods were practically unknown, it was . . . necessary to make large plates if you wanted large pictures . . . I used plates . . . from 5 x 8 up to 20 x 24 the weight of which for a serious work amounted to two or three hundred pounds or more . . . there was nearly . . . [an equal additional] weight . . . of the various chemicals.[25]

Jackson described one project in 1873 that required back-packing, "Tom taking the camera, Coulter the plate boxes & I the chemicals, etc., in all about 100 lbs. Tom and I having about 40 each."[26] For Hayden's 1871 expedition to Yellowstone, Jackson acquired a mule and named him "Hypo." In the field, Jackson wrapped cameras, chemical boxes, and supplies in a pair of raw hides which were tied to the pack saddle, and on top of this he lashed the water supply. Jackson and his group of three to five assistants and camp men called themselves the "Photographic Flying Brigade."[27]

Bringing unusually large cameras into the wilderness created particularly difficult problems. Jackson, writing about his work on the Hayden survey in 1876, described how his 20 x 24-inch camera which was tied on top of the mule pack, rather than lower down, on its side, "making a very top-heavy load;" plates and chemicals were carried by another mule. He took the outfit "over some of the highest passes in the Colorado Rockies, without a mishap, but often in imminent peril on the steepest trails when it required strenuous work of all hands to keep everything right side up."[28]

During their time in the field, photographers lived in constant fear of breaking their processed glass negatives. For Jackson, this became a nightmarish reality when he served with the Hayden survey in Colorado in 1873. On the way to the Mount of the Holy Cross, one of his mules, Gimlet, strayed from its place in the train and slipped part of its pack. Colleagues who trailed behind Jackson in the column found broken plates scattered down the mountainside. Virtually all of Jackson's 11 x 14-inch negatives were broken. The distressed photographer retraced his steps and reshot all the negatives to replace the lost plates.[29]

Some pictures required positioning the camera in virtually inaccessible locations. For one particular series of a waterfall, Jackson had to set up his camera at the bottom of a ravine. To avoid carrying most of the equipment down the cliff, he erected his darkroom at its edge. After coating a plate in the darkroom, he climbed down 200 feet into the ravine with plate holder and camera, made an exposure, and then climbed back to the top to process the plate. Jackson made four round trips into the ravine, spending half a day on that one subject,[30] prompting him to comment: "The end of the day found us exhausted but very proud."[31] Because of the elaborate preparation needed for picture-taking, the number of photographs produced in any one day varied considerably. A great deal of the time was spent locating the site, setting up the darkroom and coating the plate. By using an assistant and working from just one location, Jackson found he could make as many as fourteen negatives in half a day.[32]

It was essential for portable darkrooms used in the field to be lightweight but otherwise they varied significantly in design. Jackson described his outfits as sometimes being "a box opening up with an attached hood in which I could work with hand and arms inside the darkened enclosure. More often it was a small tent lined with non-actinic light filtering material [usually orange] . . . large enough to crawl into and be covered entirely and still have elbow room [to

PHOTOGRAPHERS OF THE WEST!

The undersigned have now on hand a well-assorted stock of the

AMERICAN OPTICAL CO.'S CELEBRATED PHOTOGRAPHIC APPARATUS.

THE ONLY PERFECT

Portrait and View Camera Boxes,   Gallery and View Stands,   Retouching Frames,
Patent Glass Baths.   Printing Frames,   Plate Boxes, &c.

All brands of Albumenized Paper,   Scovill's Fancy and Common Cases,
All Sizes of Plain Paper,   Head Rests, Back Supports, &c.
S. Peck & Co.'s Union Frames, Cases, &c.,   Envelopes, Card Stock, Chemicals, &c.

ORDERS FILLED PROMPTLY AND AT LOWEST PRICES.

J. H. TESCH & CO.,
15 SPRING ST., MILWAUKEE, WISCONSIN.

"Westward the Course of Empire takes its Way," but the
Empire State is always ahead.

HENRY D. MARKS,
ROCHESTER, NEW YORK,
DEALER IN
PHOTOGRAPHIC GOODS

Voigtlander & Son's Lenses,   S. Peck & Co.'s Unrivalled Union Goods,
C. C. Harrison Lenses,   Scovill's Common and Fancy Cases,
Darlot Lenses, Globe Lenses,   Cheap Stereoscopic Outfits, &c.

AMERICAN OPTICAL CO.'S APPARATUS.

Photographers can always obtain complete outfits from one-quarter to mammoth size.
Prices as low as any other house for the quality of the goods. Cameras and Apparatus
at manufacturers' list.

FRAMES A SPECIALTY.
109

"Henry's Lake, Idaho," detail of photograph by William Henry Jackson, 1872, see page 68, figure 52A.

do the coating and processing]."[33] The orange or yellow fabric that lined these outfits permitted colored light to enter the enclosure so the photographer could see what he was doing without affecting the plate; the light-sensitive collodion coatings reacted only to blue light. These darkrooms were uncomfortable to work in, especially during the summertime. Although Jackson always sought the coolest possible setting for his darkroom, "in carrying on the manipulations inside . . . the perspiration would run from my face in such streams that great care was needed to keep the briney fluid from spoiling my plates."[34] Photographer E. O. Beaman (while on the Powell survey in 1871-72) used a bell-shaped tent, five feet high of yellow cloth with a green fabric lining containing a one-foot square window through which filtered yellow light.[35]

The weather and other natural conditions affected the speed of picture taking. Great patience was essential because photographers sometimes had to "wait out" spells of bad weather. Photographers in the desert regions contended with extremely dry air which shrank plate holders until they literally fell apart. Glued joints parted and were no longer light-tight, making them useless for the work. Damp plate-coatings dried too rapidly and had to be constantly protected from dust and insects which could ruin otherwise perfect images. Changes of temperature, relative humidity and altitude all varied the working characteristics of the coatings and chemicals, and photographers had to correct their formulations and exposure and processing times to compensate for these variables.

Collodion coatings, being sensitive only to blue and ultra-violet light, could "distort" tonal renditions of the subject. For example, sky areas, rich in blue, tended to become overexposed on the negative in relation to foliage and soil. Thus cloud formations, although seen by the eye, usually did not register on the plate. Distant mountain ranges became indistinct if hazy conditions prevailed and strong ultra-violet light levels were present in the atmosphere. Roaring torrents of water seemed to convert into ribbons of soft

"**Photographing in High Places,**" detail of photograph by William Henry Jackson, 1872, see page 68, figure 52B.

cotton wool in most images; here too, long exposures blurred the surface texture and eliminated the ferocity of streams and rivers.

Fresh, clean water was essential; a supply had to be brought along if none was available in the picture-taking area. Shortages tested the ingenuity of the photographer. While working on a mountainside in 1870, Jackson used the water running from melting snows, but as he climbed upward and the temperature dropped, even this source disappeared. "As a last resort we caught freshly falling snow on our rubber blankets, and when the sun came out the black rubber absorbed enough warmth to melt the snow, furnishing sufficient water."[36]

Windy conditions were avoided whenever possible—movement of foliage and long exposures created distracting, blurred masses in the picture. On exposed ridges, especially at high elevations, the wind was sometimes so strong that it shook or toppled the camera. Suspending heavy rocks from the tripod platform under the camera (between the tripod legs) usually solved this problem.

Indians

Fear of Indian attacks was an ever-present concern of expeditionary photogaphers, although there were few fatalities among western photographers. Nevertheless, those which occurred were dramatic and served as a constant warning to others in the field.

The Indian's fear of being photographed was described in 1859 by Bierstadt, who stated that the Indians were "not . . . very willing to have the brass tube of the camera pointed at them. Of course they were astonished when we showed them pictures they did not sit for, . . . the best we have taken have been obtained without . . . [their] knowledge."[37] Photographer Ridgway Glover wrote in 1866 that "some of the Sioux think photography is . . . bad medicine . . . [they] think they will die in three days, if they get their pictures taken . . . I pointed the instrument at one . . . [he] fell on the sand, and rolled himself in his blanket."[38] Perhaps the photographer should have recognized that this fear could turn to dangerous anger.[39] A short

"View from Tequa toward Moqui," by William Henry Jackson, 1875, see page 105, figure 106.

time later, after leaving the safety of "Fort Kearney" (Fort Phil Kearney, Montana Territory, now Wyoming) to take some pictures, Glover was caught by the Sioux, "scalped, killed, and horribly mutilated."[40]

In 1874, W. H. Jackson noted that Indians he tried to photograph protested "vehemently, taking hold of the camera and preventing me from either focussing or making an exposure; [they angrily told him no picture taking make] all Indians heap sick, all die, pony die, poppoose die." [sic][41]

Making Prints—Back at the Studio and in the Field

Photographic prints were usually made from negatives after expeditions returned from the field, where photographers had access to permanent, convenient darkroom facilities. Printing was a time-consuming, round-the-clock, production-type operation. As with negatives, photographers usually manufactured their own photographic paper coatings. (Partially prepared commercial papers appeared in the 1860s, but expedition photographers usually made their own papers.) Formulas varied somewhat; usually plain paper was floated on a solution of salted albumen (egg whites) and dried. Under a safelight, usually at night, the coated surface was treated with light-sensitizing chemicals and dried. The following day, the paper was sandwiched behind the negative in a glass-faced frame and exposed to sunlight. The image "printed out," gradually growing darker during exposure. When the print was sufficiently dark, it was washed, toned, fixed in hypo and washed again.

Despite the complexity of this process, Hayden asked Jackson to bring all of the printing material with him on the 1870 expedition. Jackson brought supplies for "three months' work, . . . to make 10 x 8 and stereos, . . . two hundred plates of the latter size and one hundred of the former . . . [and] the paper, cards, etc., necessary to finishing up work in the field. . . ."[42] Hayden wanted the prints done rapidly in the field,[43] so that, immediately upon his return from the expedition, he could take them to Washington and show them to influential supporters of his survey.

This was a matter of considerable importance to explorers seeking government funds for additional or continued expeditions, and those who hoped to have certain areas set aside as national reserves. Jackson's photographs taken in 1871 strongly influenced passage of legislation establishing Yellowstone as the first national park. Hayden arranged for Jackson's pictures to be exhibited in the Senate building. Senator Samuel C. Pomeroy of Kansas, who had trouble bringing his Yellowstone National Park Bill to the floor for consideration notified the Senators "there are photographs of the valley and the curiosities which Senators can see." Subsequently, the bill was passed and signed by President Grant on March 1, 1872, establishing Yellowstone National Park.[44]

Reports published by the many Federal expeditions included a wide variety of magnificent images made by scientists, artists and photographers. Often they were seen only by a small, select group of people. *The Nation* commented on this restricted circulation in 1872:

[T]*he second volume of Reports illustrating the survey of the Fortieth Parallel under Mr. Clarence King has just been published . . . we should be glad to have a part, at least, of every edition sold in open market . . . At present the volumes are rarely, if ever, to be obtained except as a matter of favor from those in authority.*[45]

Popularity of Western Photographs

Senators, however, were not the only citizens who were getting acquainted with "incontrovertible evidence" about the West through photography. Thanks to the collodion process, which permitted the making of unlimited numbers of prints, the general public also was able to view the wonders of the new territories. By far the most popular photographic form was the stereograph. These images were recorded by a twin-lens camera and dual prints were mounted on cards designed to be seen through a stereographic viewer. It offered a breath-taking, three-dimensional effect, an impression which was the next closest thing to being at the scene. These twin-image cards, sold either individually or in sets, were relatively inexpensive; an eager public bought them by the hundreds of thousands. The stereographic prints were also a bonanza for the photographers. Thanks to this huge, new market, some of them could now afford to pay their own expenses during various expeditions, and thus not further drain the often limited budgets given explorers.

By 1875, however, the Department of the Interior, recognizing the importance of making the western photographs available to the general public, published a catalog listing the regular and stereoscopic views made by Jackson and sold prints to the general public at cost.[46]

and the whole supported by metallic braces fastened to the bed. When packed for travelling the braces are unshipped, the bellows loosened, and the entire front and back removed from the bed, when all can be packed in small compass. From the mode of putting together, this box is more rigid than any other, and is so simple as to preclude all possibility of getting out of order. In case that, through accident, any part should get broken, it can readily be replaced without returning the box. Price for 8 x 10, $55.00.

Stereoscopic Boxes.

X. 4 x 7 or 4 x 8 plate for using short focus Lenses, - $25.

Y. 4 x 7 or 4 x 8 plate folding bed and extra front for using
one Lens if desired, - - - - - - 30. 35.

Z. 5 x 8 for Stereo, or single plates, can be used vertically, 30. 35.

We append a cut of our improved Swing-back Success camera-box, Z, which will show at a glance its advantages and superiority over other makes. The swing-back is supported by "Wright's Patent Metallic Supports," which strengthen it, lessens the weight, and allows it to close more compactly.

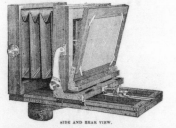

SIDE AND REAR VIEW.

In this, as well as in all our stereo-boxes, the partition can be removed and the box reversed on the tripod, for using the 5 x 8 plate vertically as well as horizontally. From the favor with which this box has been received by the trade, we predict a rapid victory over every other style of stereoscopic camera in use.

"**U.S. Geological Survey en route**," detail of photograph by William Henry Jackson, 1871, see page 58, figure 37A.

Federal Surveys

Western expansion of the frontier increased the need for more information about the vast areas of the West. As a result, when the Civil War ended, the federal government planned a series of major scientific surveys which were undertaken in the period of 1867-1878. The first of these, the U.S. Geological Exploration of the Fortieth Parallel, was established in 1867 and headed by Clarence King who selected O'Sullivan as the photographer. An outstanding legacy of graphic documentation was produced by these surveys which included the U.S. Geological and Geographical Surveys of the Territories led by F. V. Hayden; the U.S. Geophysical and Geological Survey of the Rocky Mountain Region, headed by John Wesley Powell; and the U.S. Geographical Surveys West of the One Hundredth Meridian, commanded by Lt. G. M. Wheeler.

When Congress established the U. S. Geological Survey in 1879, it merged many of the functions of the four earlier Federally-sponsored geological and geographical surveys of territories in the West that had been led by Hayden, King, Powell, and Wheeler. The new agency was made responsible for the "classification of the public lands and examination of the geological structure, mineral resources, and products of the national domain." The West would soon be as visually familiar to Americans as New England. Photographers, as well as artists and illustrators played an important role in reaching this goal. These photographs preserve the rich heritage of the West as it appeared before modern man established his imprint.

NOTES

1 Edwin James, *Account of an Expedition from Pittsburgh to the Rocky Mountains, Performed in the Years 1819 and '20 Under the Command of Major Stephen H. Long,* Vol. I (Philadelphia: H. C. Carey and I. Lea, 1823), p. 3.

2 James, Vol. II, p. 330.

3 "The Domes of the Yo Semite," *The Nation: A Weekly Journal,* Vol. IV, No. 97 (New York: E. L. Godkin & Co., May 9, 1867), pp. 379-80.

4 Clarence King, *Mountaineering in the Sierra Nevada,* ed. Francis P. Farquhar (New York: W. W. Norton & Co., 1872, reprinted 1935), p. 223.

5 Robert Taft, *Photography and the American Scene* (New York: Macmillan Co., 1938, reprinted by Dover Publications, New York, 1964), pp. 261-2 (ref: 36th Congress, First Session, Executive Document No. 56 (1860), pp. 37 and 103).

6 S[olomon] N[uñes] Carvalho, *Incidents of Travel and Adventure in the Far West; with Col. Frémont's Last Expedition* (New York: Derby and Jackson, 1857), p. 77.

7 Jesse Benton Frémont, "Some Account of the Plates," in John Charles Frémont *Memoirs of My Life . . . together with a sketch of the life of Senator Benton, in connection with Western expansion, by Jesse Benton Frémont, A retrospect of fifty years . . . Vol. 1* (Chicago and New York: Belford, Clarke & Co., 1887), p. xvi.

8 John Ross Dix, *Amusing and Thrilling Adventures of a California Artist* (Boston: Geo. E. Snow, Pathfinder Printing, 1854) pp. 1-93.

9 Dix, pp. 38-49, extracts from various newspapers.

10 Dix, p. 32.

11 Lt. Joseph C. Ives, *Report Upon the Colorado River of the West Explored in 1857 and 1858* (Washington, D.C.: U.S. Government Printing Office, 1861) pp. 32-34.

12 F. W. Lander, "Maps and Reports of the Ft. Kearney South Pass, and Honey Lake Wagon Road, for 1859 . . . 36th Cong., 2nd Session . . . No. 64 . . . Ltr. Acting Sec. of Interior," pp. 1-5.

13 John Samson, "Photographs from the High Rockies," *Harper's New Monthly Magazine,* Vol. 39 (Sept. 1869) pp. 465-475.

14 F[erdinand] V[andeveer] Hayden, *Sun Pictures of Rocky Mountain Scenery, With a Description of the Geographical and Geological Features, and Some Account of the Resources of the Great West; Containing Thirty Photographic Views along the Line of the Pacific Rail Road, From Omaha to Sacramento* (New York: Julius Bien, 1870), p. vii.

15 J[osiah] D[wight] Whitney, *The Yosemite Book; a description of the Yosemite Valley and adjacent region of the Sierra Nevada, and of the big trees of California* (New York: Julius Bien, 1868).

16 Hayden, pp. vii and viii.

17 Interview with Jacob Kainen, former Supervisor, Division of Graphic Arts, Smithsonian Institution, Washington, D.C., June 19, 1980.

18 N. P. Langford, "The Wonders of Yellowstone," *Scribner's Monthly,* Vol. II, No. 1(May 1871), pp. 1-17; Vol. II, No. 2 (July 1871), pp. 113-128.

19 William Henry Jackson, *Time Exposure: The Autobiography of William Henry Jackson* (New York: G. P. Putnam's Sons, 1940), p. 196.

20 William Henry Jackson, *Address of Mr. William Henry Jackson at the Witenagemote Club, Detroit, Michigan* (Washington, D.C.: National Anthropological Archives, Smithsonian Institution, Nov. 2, 1917), p. 17.

21 George M. Wheeler, *Progress Report Upon Geographical and Geological Explorations and Surveys West of the 100th Meridian in 1872* (Washington, D.C.: U.S. Government Printing Office, 1874), pp. 168-171, U.S. National Archives and Records Service, Record Group 57.

22 George Washington Wilson, "On Out-Door Photography," *Philadelphia Photographer,* Vol. 6, No. 61 (January 1869), pp. 66-68.

23 Robert Taft, personal communication from W. H. Jackson in *Photography and the American Scene: A Social History, 1839-1889* (New York: Macmillan, 1938, reprinted by Dover Publications, New York, 1964), p. 310.

24 Clarence King, [Memorandum] "Photographic Instruments and Materials Required for Geological Exploration of the 40th Parallel," to Maj. Gen. A. A. Humphreys, April 16, 1867. Microfilm M622, Roll 3, Record Group 57, National Archives and Records Service, Washington, D.C.

25 Jackson, *Address,* p. 12.

26 William Henry Jackson, *The Diaries of William Henry Jackson . . . 1866-67; . . . 1873 . . . and 1974,* ed. LeRoy and Ann Hafen (Glendale, Cal.: The Arthur H. Clark Co., 1959), p. 250.

27 William Henry Jackson, *The Photographic World,* Vol. I, 1871, pp. 72-73.

28 Jackson, *Address,* p. 13.

29 Jackson, *The Diaries,* pp. 242 and 243; and *Time Exposure,* p. 215.

30 William H. Jackson in collaboration with Howard R. Driggs, *The Pioneer Photographer: Rocky Mountain Adventures with a Camera* (Yonkers-on-Hudson, N.Y.: World Book Co., 1929), p. 112.

31 Jackson, *Time Exposure,* p. 199.

32 Jackson, *The Diaries,* p. 229.

33 Jackson, *Address,* p. 2.

34 Jackson, *Address,* p. 32.

35 E. O. Beaman, "Among the Aztecs, Colorado River, Arizona, Sept. 15, 1872," *Anthony's Photographic Bulletin,* Vol. III (November 1872), p. 746.

36 Jackson, *Address,* p. 16.

37 *The Crayon,* Vol. 6 (1859), p. 287.

38 Ridgway Glover, "Photography Among the Indians," *The Philadelphia Photographer,* Vol. III, No. 32 (August 1866), pp. 239-240.

39 Glover, p. 339.

40 "Obituary [of Ridgway Glover]," *The Philadelphia Photographer,* Vol. III No. 36 (December 1866), p. 371.

41 Jackson, *The Diaries,* p. 290.

42 William Henry Jackson, "Field Work," *The Philadelphia Photographer,* Vol. XII, No. 135 (March 1875), pp. 91-93.

43 Jackson and Driggs, *The Pioneer Photographer,* p. 97.

44 *The Congressional Globe,* 42nd Congress, 2nd Session, Jan. 23, 1872, p. 520.

45 Editorial, *The Nation: A Weekly Journal,* Feb. 15, 1872, p. 110.

46 William Henry Jackson, *Descriptive Catalog of The Photographs of The United States Geological Survey of The Territories for the Years 1869 to 1875 Inclusive* (Washington, D.C.: U.S. Government Printing Office, 1875); and Jackson, "Photographs of Rocky Mountain Scenery, and its Prehistoric Ruins," *Anthony's Photographic Bulletin* (1876), p. 187.

PORTFOLIO

Picture titles in quotation marks usually refer to captions or imprints on images or their mounts; original spelling and punctuation are preserved. Titles found elsewhere are so noted. Images are photographic albumen prints unless otherwise specified. Dimensions are given in inches; height precedes width.

1. "Robinson's Landing, Mouth of Colorado River"

Monochrome lithograph from a drawing by J. J. Young based on a wet-plate photograph by 1st Lt. Joseph Christmas Ives, 1857. Stop-action photography was not possible during this early period of photography. The moving figures were added by the artist.

Published in Ives, *Report upon the Colorado River of the West* (Washington: Government Printing Office, 1861).

By Sarony, Major & Knapp
5¾″ x 8¾″
From Smithsonian Institution Libraries

2A. "Crabs Claw Peak, Andesite Columns, Western Nevada"

Rhyolite columnals forming part of "Karnak Ridge," near present Ragged Top Mountain, Trinity Range (called "Montezuma Range" by King survey), Pershing County, Nevada. "Karnak" was named for its resemblance to the multi-columned Egyptian temple (Rabbitt, p. 165). Alternate title: "Volcanic Ridge, Trinity Mountains (Nevada)" (Naef, pl. 37)

$7\frac{7}{8}''$ x $10\frac{11}{16}''$ on $11\frac{3}{8}''$ x 14" mount
From U. S. Geological Survey

2B. "Columnar Rhyolite—Karnak—Nevada"

Toned lithograph by Julius Bien (note the clouds which have been added by the artist to this and other lithographs in this catalog).

From Arnold Hague and S. F. Emmons, *Descriptive Geology,* Vol. II of Clarence King, *Report of the Geological Exploration of the Fortieth Parallel,* Washington: Government Printing Office, 1877, Plate XXIII.

$5\frac{3}{4}''$ x $8\frac{1}{4}''$
From Smithsonian Institution Libraries

2C. "The Carson Sink"

Wood engraving from *Harper's New Monthly Magazine,* September 1869, p. 470. The figures, not in the original photograph, were added by the wood engraver.

5" x $4\frac{3}{8}''$
From Smithsonian Institution Libraries

4. "Castellated Rocks on the Chugwater"
Valley of Chugwater Creek, southeast
Wyoming, possibly Laramie County.
Sanford Robinson Gifford was photo-
graphed while painting "Valley of
the Chug Water Wyoming Ter.," the
scene shown in fig. 3. By William
Henry Jackson (Hayden survey),
August 9, 1870 (the date on the
Gifford painting). From 1870 series
(6½″ x 8½″ negatives), No. 50
(Jackson catalog, p. 11).
5″ x 7¾″ on 11″ x 14″ mount
From Denver Public Library

3. "Vally of the Chug Water Wyoming Ter."
(See fig. 4)
Oil on canvas by Sanford Robinson
Gifford, 1870
8¼" x 13⅜"
From the Amon Carter Museum

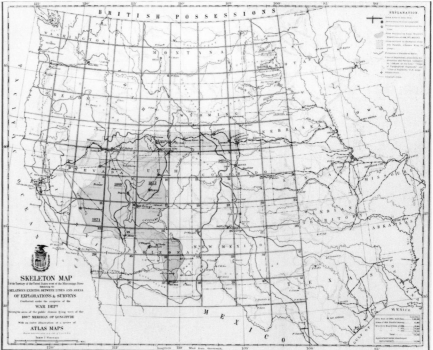

5. "Skeleton Map of the Territory of the United States west of the Mississippi River

Exhibiting the Relations Existing Between Lines and Areas of Explorations & Surveys Conducted under the auspices of the War Department. Giving the area of the public domain lying west of the 100th Meridian . . ." Scale 1:6,000,000.

Map from George M. Wheeler, *Progress-Report upon Geographical and Geological Explorations and Surveys, West of the One Hundredth Meridian, in 1872,* Washington: Government Printing Office, 1874, opp. p. 43

By American Photo-lithographic Company, New York (Osborne's Process)
16½" x 21"
From Smithsonian Institution Libraries

6. "Ancient Ruins in the Cañon de Chelle, N. M./In a niche 50 feet above present Cañon bed"

"White House" ruins, west Canyon de Chelle, Canyon de Chelle National Monument, Apache County, Arizona

By Timothy H. O'Sullivan (Wheeler survey), 1873

From 1873 O'Sullivan series, mount imprinted No. 11 (No. 10 in Wheeler, *Photographs . . .* 1873)

14″ x 11″ on 19½″ x 15¾″ mount
From Denver Public Library

7A. "Old Pueblo Ruins, Cañon de Chelle, N.M."

Stereograph by Timothy H. O'Sullivan (Wheeler survey), 1873

4″ x 7″

From Division of Photographic History, Smithsonian Institution

7B. "Ruins of an old Pueblo/in the Cañon of Chelly—Sept. 8th"

This drawing was done more than a decade before photography played a role in documenting the Far West. Also see fig. 8B.

Lithograph by R. H. Kern from J. E. Johnston and others, *Reports of the Secretary of War, with Reconnaissances of Routes from San Antonio to El Paso . . .* Washington, 1850, Plate 53

7¼″ x 4⁵⁄₁₆″

From Smithsonian Institution Libraries

8A. "Zuni, Looking S.E." (in negative)

View from Zuni Pueblo Looking east-southeast toward "Taaiyalone Mountain" (now called "Dowa Yalanne" mesa), McKinley County, New Mexico

By John K. Hillers for the Smithsonian Institution's Bureau of Ethnology, ca. 1879 or later

9⅞" x 12⅞" on 16" x 20" mount

From Denver Public Library

8B. "Pueblo of Zuni/Sept. 15"

Lithograph by R. H. Kern from J. E. Johnston and others, *Reports of the Secretary of War with Reconnaissances of Routes from San Antonio to El Paso . . .* Washington, 1850, Plate 59

4⅜" x 7¼"

From Smithsonian Institution Libraries

9. "Virgin River Valley, Utah" (pencil under image)

Probably the southeast face of the Towers of the Virgin, including the West Temple, the Three Marys and Meridian Tower, Zion National Park, Washington County, Utah

By John K. Hillers (Powell survey), 1872 or later

9¾" x 12⅞" on 16" x 20" mount

From U. S. Geological Survey

10. "Green R near Flaming Gorge" (ink on mount)

Horseshoe Canyon, Green River, south of Flaming Gorge, Daggett County, Utah

By Timothy H. O'Sullivan (King survey), 1868

8″ x 10⅝″ on 16″ x 20″ mount
From The Library of Congress

11. "Horse Shoe Curve—Green River—Wyoming"

Toned lithograph by Julius Bien from O'Sullivan photograph above. From Arnold Hague and S. F. Emmons, *Descriptive Geology*, Vol. II of Clarence King, *Report of the Geological Exploration of the Fortieth Parallel*, Washington: Government Printing Office, 1877, Plate I
5⅞″ x 8½″
From Smithsonian Institution Libraries

12A. "Three Patriarchs, West Side of Zion Canyon"

South face of the "Three Patriarchs," Zion National Park, Washington County, Utah

By John K. Hillers, probably on the Powell survey, 1872 or later.

9⅞″ x 13″ on 16″ x 20″ mount
From U.S. Geological Survey

12B. "'Three Tétons,' Looking East"

Wood engraving based on sketch by William Henry Holmes. Art work was used to highlight specific features of a subject as in this engraving which might have been traced or copied from a photograph.

From F. V. Hayden, *Sixth Annual Report of the United States Geological Survey of the Territories ... Explorations for the Year 1872*, Washington: Government Printing Office, 1873, Fig. 47
3″ x 7¼″
From Smithsonian Institution Libraries

13A. "The Pike's Peak Group/From Bluff East of Monument Creek" (Colorado)

Lithograph by Julius Bien from F. V. Hayden, *Geological and Geographical Atlas of Colorado and Portions of Adjacent Territory,* 1877, Sheet XIX

5⅛" x 34⅛"

From Smithsonian Institution Libraries

13B. Untitled

Five pages of pencil drawings by William Henry Holmes, forming panoramic view from which the lithograph above was drawn. The pages are from Holmes' sketch book for the Hayden survey in Colorado, 1874, Field Notebook No. 1170. Lithograph in 13A is also based on these drawings, which bear notations by the artist about colors (see enlargement) and other information to serve as guides for doing subsequent versions (such as the lithograph). Holmes also did some fanciful "doodling," shaping heads in the mountainsides (see enlargement). Also see fig. 13D.

Each sheet, 7" x 11¾"; total panorama, 7" x 59"

From the National Archives and Records Service

13C. "Central Portions of the Elk Mountains/Looking West" (Colorado)
Lithograph by Julius Bien, from same sheet as fig. 13A
5⅛″ x 34⅛″
From Smithsonian Institution Libraries

13D. Untitled
Four pages of pencil drawings by William Henry Holmes, forming a panoramic view from which the lithograph, fig. 13C, was drawn. The pages are from the same sketch book as fig. 13B.
Each sheet, 7″ x 11¾″; total panorama, 7″ x 47½″
From the National Archives and Records Service

14A. Untitled
Shoshone Falls, Idaho
By Timothy H. O'Sullivan (King
survey), 1868. "74" in negative.
12⅝″ x 14¾″ on 18¹⁄₁₆″ x 24¹⁄₁₆″ mount
From Denver Public Library

14B. "Shoshone Falls—Idaho—From Above"

Lithograph (copied from the photograph shown in fig. 14A) by Julius Bien. From Clarence King, *Systematic Geology*, Vol. I of *Report of the Geological Exploration of the Fortieth Parallel*, Washington: Government Printing Office, 1878, Plate XVIII.

5⅞″ x 8⅜″

From Smithsonian Institution Libraries

14C. "Above the Shoshone Falls"

Wood engraving from *Harper's New Monthly Magazine*, September 1869, p. 474

3½″ x 4½″

From Smithsonian Institution Libraries

15A. "Grand Cañon of the Colorado River, Mouth of Kanab Wash; Looking West"

Actually, view is south down the Colorado River from the west side of Marble Canyon, north of the mouth of Soap Creek, Coconino County, Arizona.

By William Bell (Wheeler survey), 1872

1872 series, No. 13
14″ x 11″ on 20″ x 16¹⁄₁₆″ mount
From Denver Public Library

15B. "Marble Cañon (1200 feet deep), Colorado"
Stereograph by William Bell (Wheeler survey), 1872
4″ x 7″
From Denver Public Library

15C. "Marble Cañon/Colorado River"
Toned lithograph by the Graphic Company, New York City, from G. M. Wheeler, *Report upon Geographical and Geological Explorations and Surveys, West of the One Hundredth Meridian . . . Vol. III — Geology,* Washington: Government Printing Office, 1875, Plate II.
7¹³⁄₁₆″ x 5¹³⁄₁₆″
From Smithsonian Institution Libraries

16. "Upper Geyser Basin—Firehole River"

Watercolor on paper, Yellowstone National Park, Wyoming. By John H. Renshawe, 1883

6¾″ x 9⅝″

From Yellowstone National Park, National Park Service

17. "The Beehive Group of Geysers/ Yellowstone Park" (in negative)

Upper Geyser Basin

Probably by William Henry Jackson, either 1878 (Hayden survey), or 1883 or 1885 for W. H. Jackson & Co., Denver, but photographer identified as "Jack Hillers, ca. 1880" in Goetzmann, p. 610.

10⅞″ x 13⅜″ on 11″ x 14″ mount

From Denver Public Library

THE BEE HIVE GROUP OF GEYSERS
YELLOWSTONE PARK

18B. "Lower Fall of Yellowstone River"
Wood engraving, signed "J. D. Woodward," lower right, and "T. Cotefu"(?), lower left. From F. V. Hayden, *Sixth Annual Report of the United States Geological Survey of the Territories . . . 1872,* Washington: Government Printing Office, 1873, fig. 34, opposite p. 132
8³⁄₁₆″ x 4½″
From Smithsonian Institution Libraries.

18A. "Lower Fall/Yellowstone"
Pencil on paper, by Charles Moore, 1870 (signed "Moore," lower left). The abilities and talents of illustrators and artists who documented the West varied considerably. Compare this image with fig. 18B.
7″ x 5½″
From Yellowstone National Park, National Park Service

19. "Tower Falls"
Watercolor on paper, Yellowstone National Park, Wyoming
By John H. Renshawe, 1883
9⅞″ x 5½″
From Yellowstone National Park, National Park Service

20. Untitled
Bridal Veil Falls, Yosemite, California
By Carleton E. Watkins, 1861
3⅝″ x 4¾″ on 8¾″ x 10⅝″ mount
From The Library of Congress

21A. "Camp No. 4 Near Promontory Point Great Salt Lake"

Lithograph by Ackerman, from Howard Stansbury, *Exploration and Survey of the Valley of the Great Salt Lake of Utah*, Philadelphia, 1852, opposite p. 169. Western landscape art "was often somewhat contrived to emphasize the inspirational effect of the scene . . . with artists selecting and ordering the appearance of nature to concur with their individual attitudes" (Truettner, p. 21).

4½″ x 7⅞″

From Smithsonain Institution Libraries

21B. "Rainbow Falls, Yosemite Valley"
Color halftone copy of a painting by
Thomas Moran, 1905
11⁹⁄₁₆″ x 8¼″, unmounted
From Denver Public Library

**21C. "Cliffs of the Upper Colorado
River, Wyoming Territory"**
Chromolithograph by L. Prang &
Co., 1881, after a painting by Thomas
Moran
12³⁄₁₆″ x 7¹⁄₁₆″, unmounted
From Denver Public Library

22A. "Mountain of the Holy Cross, in the Great National Range of Colorado"

Mount of the Holy Cross (elevation 14,003 ft.), Sawatch Range, Eagle County, Colorado. Originally entitled "The Mount of the Holy Cross," no. 106 in Jackson's 1873 series (11″ x 14″ negatives), this print may have been retitled by W. H. Jackson & Co. (see Jackson catalog, p. 60; also Prof. J. D. Whitney's letter concerning the expedition to the Mount, pp. 60-62; and 1873 series [5″ x 8″ negatives], No. 60, p. 64; and 1873 stereoscopic series, No. 718, p. 65).

By William Henry Jackson (Hayden survey), August 24, 1873
9⅛″ x 13¹⁄₁₆″ on 15″ x 19½″ mount
From U.S. Geological Survey

22B. "El Monte de la Santa Cruz"
Wood engraving published in unidentified magazine, late 19th century, after a photograph by "W. H. Jackson P. & P. Co."
6⅞″ x 4¼″, unmounted
From Denver Public Library

22C. "Mount of the Holy Cross"
Hand-tinted silver (gelatin?) print by unidentified photographer, late 19th or early 20th century
7½″ x 3⅝″, unmounted
From Division of Photographic History, Smithsonian Institution

22D. "The Mountain of the Holy Cross Colorado"
Chromolithograph by L. Prang after painting by Thomas Moran, n.d.
14″ x 9¾″, unmounted
From Denver Public Library

23A. Untitled

Cascade, Provo Canyon, possibly of
the "Upper Falls," looking southeast,
south side of Provo Canyon, Wasatch
Range, Utah County, Utah. A tiny
figure (see enlargement) is included
for scale in lower center portion of
photograph.

By Timothy H. O'Sullivan (King
survey), 1868, or 1869

7⅞″ x 10⅝″ on 11½″ x 14″ mount

From U.S. Geological Survey

**23B. "Provo Fall—Wasatch Range—
Utah"**
Toned lithograph from Clarence
King, *Systematic Geology,* Vol. I of
*Report of the Geological Exploration of
the Fortieth Parallel,* Washington:
Government Printing Office, 1878,
Plate X. Note how the figure is
emphasized in the lithograph.
5″ x 8½″
From Smithsonian Institution
Libraries

25A. "View of Yosemite Valley from Inspiration Point, This/Point is 1,427 ft. above the Floor of the Valley"

Silver gelatin print, photographer unidentified

3½″ x 10⅞″, unmounted

From Denver Public Library

25B. "The Yosemite Valley, from the Mariposa Trail, Yosemite Valley, Mariposa Co., Cal."

Stereograph, No. 1137 from *Watkins' Pacific Coast Series*

By Carleton E. Watkins, 1860s

3½″ x 7″

From Denver Public Library

24. Untitled

Pencil and chalk, South Fork, Valley of the Yosemite. The King and Gardner topographical map of 1865 depicts an "Illilouette or South Fork" (Merced River); it is known as Illilouette Creek on U.S. Geological Survey maps. Series, figs. 24-29, showing same general area as illustrated by artists and photographers.

By Thomas A. Ayres, 1855

On composition board, 13¼″ x 20½″

From Yosemite National Park, National Park Service

26. Untitled
Yosemite Valley, California
Possibly by Carleton E. Watkins,
1860s
14⅞″ x 20″ on 20½″ x 27⁹⁄₁₆″ mount
From Denver Public Library

27. "View of Yosemite Valley"
Oil on canvas by Thomas Hill, n.d.
(signed "T. Hill," lower left)
26¾″ x 33¾″
From Yosemite National Park,
National Park Service

28A. "View up the Valley, from the foot of the Mariposa Trail,/Yosemite Valley, Mariposa County, Cal."
Stereograph, No. 1001 from *Watkins' Pacific Coast Series*
By Carleton E. Watkins, 1860s
3⁷⁄₁₆″ x 7″
From Denver Public Library

28B. "Yosemite Valley from Bridal Veil Meadows" (California)
By George Fiske, 1885
4¼″ x 7¼″
From Division of Photographic History, Smithsonian Institution

29. Untitled
El Capitan and the Cathedral Group, Yosemite Valley, California. Reproduced in Naef, plate 8, captioned: "Up the Valley from the Mariposa Trail—El Capitan and the Cathedral Group, Yosemite No. 9."
By Carleton E. Watkins, ca. 1866
15¾″ x 20⅝″ on 20⁵⁄₁₆″ x 27⅝″ mount
From Denver Public Library

30. Untitled
Yosemite Falls, California
By Carleton E. Watkins (signed "C. E. Watkins," lower right under print), ca. 1866
16⅝″ x 20⅝″ on 21″ x 25¹⁄₁₆″ mount
From Denver Public Library

31. "Yosemite Falls"
Pencil and chalk by Thomas A. Ayres, 1855
On composition board, 19½″ x 13¾″
From Yosemite National Park, National Park Service

32. "The Crested Hot Spring and the Castle" (in negative)
Castle Geyser and hot spring, Upper Geyser Basin, Yellowstone National Park
By William Henry Jackson ("W.H.J." in negative, lower left), either 1878 (Hayden survey), 1883, or 1885
17¼″ x 21″ on 18⅜″ x 21⁷⁄₁₆″ mount
From U.S. Geological Survey

34. "Excelsior Geyser and Prismatic Springs, Midway Basin"
From "Bluff Point" (1878 map feature), west across the Firehole River toward the Grand Prismatic Spring (background at left), Midway Geyser Basin, Yellowstone National Park. Similar view (Albertype?) entitled "Cliff Cauldron/Egeria Springs," in article by Peale in Hayden, *12th Annual Report for 1878* (1883), Plate XIII.

By William Henry Jackson (?), 1878 (Hayden survey), or 1883 or 1885 for W. H. Jackson & Co., Denver
9½″ x 13⅛″ on 16″ x 20″ mount
From Denver Public Library ▶

33. "Castle Geyser"
Yellowstone National Park, Wyoming
Watercolor on paper by John H. Renshawe, 1883
6⅞″ x 9⅞″
From Yellowstone National Park, National Park Service

35. "Excelsior Geyser, Yellowstone Park" (Wyoming)
Watercolor on paper by Thomas Moran, 1873
12¾″ x 9¾″
From the National Museum of American Art, Smithsonian Institution; gift of Mrs. Peter Armistead, Jr.

EXCELSIOR GEYSER AND PRISMATIC SPRINGS, MIDWAY BASIN.

36. "North from Berthoud Pass"

Berthoud Pass (elevation 11,315 ft.), Gilpin County, Colorado. Jackson said the view was made from a point about 800 feet above the lowest point of the pass, and identified James Peak "near the center" (probably just to right of center in the background). The figure is Harry Yount, a hunter with the Hayden survey from 1873, and later the first ranger in Yellowstone National Park.

By William Henry Jackson (Hayden survey), 1874 series (5″ x 8″ negatives), No. 65 (Jackson catalog, p. 66)
4⅜″ x 7¼″ on 11″ x 14″ mount
From Denver Public Library

37B. "The Odometer"

Albertype photomechanical print, probably at or near the Hayden survey camp, Mirror Lake, Yellowstone National Park. The operator of the odometer (a device for measuring mileage in meander surveying) is probably Edward Goodfellow (see description of the odometer in the Jackson catalog, p. 31: ". . . first wheels that were ever taken into this little-known region").

By William Henry Jackson (Hayden survey), 1871 series (8″ x 10″ negatives), No. 301. By E. Bierstadt from Jackson photograph
7½″ x 9¼″ image on 11″ x 14¹/₁₆″ sheet
From Denver Public Library

37A. "U.S. Geological Survey en route"

Hayden survey members probably along the shore of Shadow Lake, between Pelican Creek and Lamar River, Yellowstone National Park. The figures at the head of the pack train, from the right, are 2nd Lt. Gustavus C. Doane (2d Cavalry Rgt., Ft. Ellis), Ferdinand Vandeveer Hayden, James Stevenson, Anton Schönborn, and Edward Goodfellow with his odometer cart.

By William Henry Jackson (Hayden survey), 1871 series (8″ x 10″ negatives), No. 303 (Jackson catalog, p. 31; see also Jackson and Driggs, p. 119)
6½″ x 8¾″ on 11″ x 13⅞″ mount
From U.S. Geological Survey

38A. "Fred Loring and His Mule 'Evil Merodach'"

Stereograph, probably at or near Camp Mohave, on the east side of the Colorado River, near Beal's Crossing, in present Mohave County, Arizona. Loring served with the Wheeler survey as a "barometric observer and recorder" and as a writer/reporter for *Appleton's;* he and two other Wheeler men were killed by Apache Mohaves (?) in the "Wickenburg Massacre" stage hold-up, November 5, 1871. On Loring, see Horan, pp. 238-240, 245, 252-254.

By Timothy H. O'Sullivan (Wheeler survey), late October or early November 1871

4″ x 7″

From Denver Public Library

38B. "John, the cook, baking slapjacks" (in pencil on reverse; also in catalog)

Stereograph, "Potato John" Raymond cooking flapjacks. The flapjack in mid-air was painted in the negative; required exposures were too long for stop-action photography.

By William Henry Jackson (Hayden survey), 1874 stereoscopic series, No. 842 (Jackson catalog, p. 74)

4″ x 7″

From the Colorado Historical Society

38C. "Inquiring for the Water Pocket"

Stereograph, John Wesley Powell with an Indian of the "Kai-vav-its" tribe of the "Pai Utes," near the Grand Canyon of the Colorado, Arizona

By John K. Hillers (Powell survey), 1873. Published by J. F. Jarvis

4½″ x 7″

From Division of Photographic History, Smithsonian Institution

38D. "Sinching the Aparejo" (title in Jackson catalog)

Stereograph; photographs were sometimes taken for instructional purposes, such as this series on packing a mule, figs. 38D-38F, from *Views among the Rocky Mountains of Colorado* (see Jackson catalog, 1874 stereoscopic series, Nos. 835-841, pp. 73-74).

"837" in negative

By William Henry Jackson (Hayden survey), 1874

4″ x 7″

From the Colorado Historical Society

38E. "Packing, putting up the load" (title in Jackson catalog)

Stereograph, by William Henry Jackson (Hayden survey), 1874 (Jackson catalog, No. 838, p. 74)

4″ x 7″

From Denver Public Library

38F. "Packing, sinching" (title in Jackson catalog)

"839" in negative

Stereograph by William Henry Jackson (Hayden survey), 1874

4″ x 7″

From Denver Public Library

39. "Jose and Joe Clark, Hunters of U.S.G.S."

Probably at or near the Hayden survey camp, Mirror Lake, Yellowstone National Park. The hunters are carrying elk meat.

By William Henry Jackson (Hayden survey), 1871 series (8″ x 10″ negatives), No. 302 (Jackson catalog, p. 31. *Cf.* 1871 stereoscopic series, No. 463, p. 34)

6⅞″ x 8⅞″ on 11″ x 14″ mount
From Denver Public Library

40. "Under the Upper Yo Semite Falls" (California)

A surveyor and his equipment are shown.

By Carleton E. Watkins, ca. 1870
3⅝″ x 4¾″ on 8¾″ x 10⅝″ mount
From The Library of Congress

41. Untitled

The astronomical observatory, South Ruby Valley, near Fort Ruby, in present White Pine County, Nevada. Shown in front of the tent are a zenith telescope (right), meridian telescope (center), and telegraph (left).

By Timothy H. O'Sullivan (King survey), 1868 series No. 42

7¾" x 10⅝" on 12⅜" x 14½" mount

From U.S. Geological Survey

42. Untitled

Kansas Pacific Survey members and covered wagon in Colorado
By Dr. William A. Bell, 1867

Dr. William A. Bell was an English physician, *not* to be confused with the William Bell of the Wheeler survey. See chapter on Dr. Bell in *Current,* pp. 48-55. This photograph reproduced as "Camp Scene along the 32nd Parallel, Kansas-Pacific Survey, 1867," p. 55.

4¼" x 5½" oval on 6¹/₁₆" x 7³/₁₆" mount

From the Colorado Historical Society

43A. "Expedition of 1870"

Members of the Hayden survey in camp on the flats of Bessemer Bend of the North Platte River, near Red Buttes, Natrona County, Wyoming. The figures are: sitting, left to right, Charles S. Turnbull, John H. Beaman, Ferdinand Vandeveer Hayden, Cyrus Thomas, Raphael (a hunter), and Arthur L. Ford; standing, left to right, two cooks, Sanford Robinson Gifford, Henry Wood Elliott, James Stevenson, Henry D. Schmidt [Schmitt], E. Campbell Carrington, Lester A. Bartlett, and William Henry Jackson. See Jackson catalog, p. 14; also *cf.* 1870 stereoscopic series, No. 303, p. 20. Survey members' identification in Jackson and Driggs, p. 82.

By William Henry Jackson (Hayden survey), August 24, 1870. From 1870 series (6½″ x 8½″ negatives), No. 80
5″ x 7⅞″ on 11″ x 14″ mount
From Denver Public Library

43B. "Hayden Camp"

Wood engraving from *Frank Leslie's Illustrated Newspaper,* August 22, 1874, based on Jackson photograph
Clipping mounted on cardboard, 8⅜″ x 10⅜″
From U.S. Geological Survey

44A. Untitled

Humboldt Hot Springs, probably present Dixie Hot Springs, in Dixie Valley (called "Osobb Valley" by the King survey), near the east slope of the Stillwater Range, Churchill County, Nevada. O'Sullivan's equipment wagon and photographic outfit are shown.

By Timothy H. O'Sullivan (King survey), probably 1868

7¾″ x 10⅝″ on 12⅜″ x 14¾″ mount
From U.S. Geological Survey

44B. "Sou Springs—Osobb Valley—Nevada"

Toned lithograph from Hague and Emmons, *Descriptive Geology,* 1877, Plate XX. Photographic outfit shown at left in fig. 44A (see enlargement) has been retouched out of this litho—graph. The retouching can be seen in original with a 10X magnifier, indicating that the Bien prints are, in fact, photolithographs (see Kainen, text citation No. 17).

5⅞″ x 8½″
From Smithsonian Institution Libraries

44C. Untitled

Baker's wood engraving of John Carbutt's "portable developing box" (plate coating/processing outfit for the collodion process), from *The Philadelphia Photographer,* January 1865, p. 5.

3″ x 4½″
From Smithsonian Institution Libraries.

45A. "Black Cañon, Colorado River, from Camp 8, Looking Above"

Upstream from the west bank of the Colorado River, standpoint located in Clark County, California. O'Sullivan's boat, *Picture,* in left foreground; note photographic equipment in bow.

By Timothy H. O'Sullivan (Wheeler survey), ca. Sept. 23, 1871
8″ x 10¾″ on 11⅜″ x 14¼″ mount
From U.S. Geological Survey

45B. "Black Cañon, Colorado River, from Camp 8, Looking Above/1871"

Toned photolithograph by Julius Bien, From George M. Wheeler, *Report upon United States Geographical Surveys West of the One Hundredth Meridian . . . Vol. I—Geographical Report,* Washington: Government Printing Office, 1889, Plate XVII.
5¹⁵⁄₁₆″ x 8½″
From Smithsonian Institution Libraries

46. "Panorama of Buffalo Peaks and Saguache Range, from Weston's Pass"

(Colorado)

Part of a panoramic series. Also titled by Jackson, "Panorama of Buffalo Peaks/South End of Park Range" (Park Range is now Mosquito Range; Saguache Range is now Sawatch Range.

By William Henry Jackson (Hayden survey), 1873 series (11″ x 14″ negatives), No. 85 (Jackson catalog, pp. 57-58)

6⅞″ x 12½″ on 15¹/₁₆″ x 19⁷/₁₆″ mount
From U.S. Geological Survey

47. "Ancient Ruins, Cañon de Chelle, N.M."

Stereograph shows artist Alexander Helwig Wyant at work.

By Timothy H. O'Sullivan (Wheeler survey), 1873
4″ x 7″
From The Library of Congress

49. "Scene in Glen Cañon, on the Colorado River of the West—Photographing a Child of Nature"

Glen Canyon divides Garfield and San Juan Counties, Utah.

Wood engraving from *Frank Leslie's Illustrated Newspaper,* December 11, 1886, possibly based on a photograph by E. O. Beaman (Powell survey), 1871

10⅞″ x 8³⁄₁₆″ image on 15⅛″ x 10⅞″ sheet

From Denver Public Library

50A. "Taking Stereoscopic Pictures of Near Objects"

Wood engraving; figs. 50A and 50B illustrate two methods of producing stereoscopic photographs: using two separate cameras spaced a few inches apart, or incorporating both lenses into one camera body.

4½″ x 2⅛″

From Smithsonian Institution Libraries

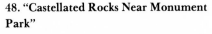

48. "Castellated Rocks Near Monument Park"

Also described by Jackson as a "Study of picturesque pine and castellated rocks, with sun shining through the branches of the tree" (Jackson catalog, p. 68).

By William Henry Jackson (Hayden survey), 1874 series (5″ x 8″ negatives), No. 120

7¼″ x 4⅜″ on 14″ x 11″ mount

From U.S. Geological Survey

50B. "Stereoscopic Camera"

Wood engraving, figs. 50A and 50B both from *Harper's New Monthly Magazine* (September 1869, p. 479)

1¹¹⁄₁₆″ x 2⅛″

From Smithsonian Institution Libraries

51A. Untitled

Stereograph, from series, *Across the Continent on the Union Pacific Railway, Eastern Division.* Note large, collapsed camera without lens, lower right.

By Alexander Gardner, between Sept. 15 and Oct. 19, 1867; published by Gardner's Photographic Art Gallery, 1868

3½″ x 7″

From Division of Photographic History, Smithsonian Institution

51B. "A rare specimen found on hill above Ft. Riley, Kansas"

Stereograph, from series, *Across the Continent on the Union Pacific Railway, Eastern Division.* Photographic darkroom is shown on wagon, tripod leans on front right wagon wheel, photographer(?) sits on camera and holds lens in lap. According to Robert Sobieszek, Gardner's pictures from this period "were the first, large scale photographic presentation of the generally uncharted terrain beyond the frontier" (Sobieszek, pp. 6-8).

By Alexander Gardner, published by Gardner's Photographic Art Gallery (dates in fig. 51A)

3½″ x 7″

From Division of Photographic History, Smithsonian Institution

51C. "Keystone Art Cabinet, Containing 400 Choice Views"

Stereograph, advertisement for Keystone stereographs, and viewing and storage systems.

By Keystone View Company, 1898 or later (Darrah, pp. 49-50). The Keystone View Co. was the last company to manufacture card stereographs, filling orders until 1970 (Darrah, p. 51).

3½″ x 7″

From Division of Photographic History, Smithsonian Institution

51D. Untitled (photographer unknown)

Stereograph, photographer with tripod-mounted stereoscopic camera, ca. 1870

3″ x 6¾″

From Division of Photographic History, Smithsonian Institution

51E. Untitled

Stereograph (with advertisement on reverse), interior of D. Appleton & Co.'s Stereoscopic Emporium, New York

Hand-held, floor, and table-model stereoscopes and related items are shown. Appleton published stereographs and was the first importer and distributor of stereographs in America (Darrah, pp. 22-23).

By D. Appleton & Co., New York, probably 1850s

3½″ x 7″

From Division of Photographic History, Smithsonian Institution

51F. "Twin Lakes, Colorado"

Stereograph, photographic outfit shown at left

Possibly by William Henry Jackson (Hayden survey), ca. 1873

3¹⁵⁄₁₆″ x 7″

From Denver Public Library

52A. "Henry's Lake, Idaho"
Stereograph, Henry's Lake looking
toward Sawtell Peak and Red Rock
Mountain (left background), Idaho.
Photographic darkroom shown on
right. Dark rectangle is translucent,
yellow or orange cloth through which
a "safe" (colored) light enters tent,
enabling photographer to work. Collodion wet plate coatings did not
react to light of these colors.
By William Henry Jackson (Hayden
survey), ca. August 8-10, 1872. From
1872 stereoscopic series, No. 531
(Jackson catalog, p. 47)
4″ x 7″
From Denver Public Library

**52B. "Photographing in High
Places"** (in negative)
William Henry Jackson, kneeling,
and his assistant Charles R.
Campbell, standing. View east-southeast toward the Teton Range, north-
west Wyoming. The Grand Teton
frames Campbell's hat.
By William Henry Jackson (Hayden
survey), late July 1872. From 1872
series (8″ x 10″ negatives), No. 423 (a
stereograph, 1872 series, No. 515, has
the same title: see Jackson catalog,
pp. 41, 42, 47)
Gelatin print exhibited, date unknown, 8¾″ x 7″ on 11″ x 8½″ mount
From U.S. Geological Survey

53. "Ranch on the Yellowstone"
(in negative)

Valley of the Yellowstone River, southeast of the present town of Miner, Park County, Montana, probably near present "Yankee Jim Canyon." Jackson described this scene as "Major Pease's Ranch on the Yellowstone River, 3 miles above the First Canon" (Jackson catalog, p. 44). Note photographic equipment and darkroom tent.

By William Henry Jackson (Hayden survey), late July 1872

1872 series (8″ x 10″ negatives), No. 469
6½″ x 8⅞″ on 11″ x 14″ mount
From U.S. Geological Survey

54. "Argentine Pass" (in negative)

View looking southeast across Argentine Pass toward Argentine Peak and Square Top Mountain. Jackson's darkroom tent is shown on left (see enlargement). Part of Jackson's "A Panoramic View of the Front Range of the Rocky Mountains, from near Gray's and Torrey's Peaks" (1873 series, Nos. 65-70); the entire panorama includes Long's Peak south to Pike's Peak.

By William Henry Jackson (Hayden survey), 1873 series (11″ x 14″ negatives), No. 69 (Jackson catalog, pp. 54-55)

9⁹⁄₁₆″ x 12⅜″ on 15¹⁄₁₆″ x 19½″ mount
From U.S. Geological Survey

69

55. **"Sand Dunes, Carson Desert, Nevada"** (ink on mount, below print)
Southwest of Carson Sink, Churchill County. O'Sullivan's supply wagon and mules are shown. (Darkroom wagons could be used wherever trails existed, but light-weight, portable units were back-packed into more inaccessible areas.)
By Timothy H. O'Sullivan (King Survey), 1868
8″ x 10⅝″ on 16″ x 20″ mount
From The Library of Congress

56. **"Shifting Sand-Mounds"**
Wood engraving from *Harper's New Monthly Magazine,* September 1869, p.474, copied from O'Sullivan photograph
2³⁄₁₆″ x 4″
From Smithsonian Institution Libraries

59A. "The Annie,/first boat ever launched on Yellowstone Lake"
By William Henry Jackson (Hayden survey), ca. July 29, 1871. From 1871 series (8″ x 10″ negatives), No. 273 (Jackson catalog, p. 29)
7½″ x 9″ on 11″ x 14″ mount
From Denver Public Library

59B. "The Anna"
Stereograph.
Note: Jackson called the boat *Anna*, although *Annie* is the name on the boat in both photographs. However, "Anna" appears on the boat in the Albertype image, 59C, which was apparently retouched. The boat was named in honor of Anna L. Dawes, a daughter of then Representative Henry L. Dawes of Massachusetts, one of Hayden's sponsors (Jackson catalog, p. 29).

From *Scenery on the Yellowstone,* 1871 By William Henry Jackson, ca. July 29, 1871 (stereoscopic series, No. 456), also identified as "Sail-boat Anna, on the Lake" (p. 34)
3¹⁵⁄₁₆″ x 7″ mount
From Denver Public Library

59C. "First Boat on Yellowstone Lake"
Bierstadt Albertype photomechanical reproduction; the process reversed the image.
5″ x 8⅞″ on 11″ x 14″ sheet
From Denver Public Library

57. "Nevada Falls, 700 ft., Yosemite" (California)

Long exposures eliminated any possibility of capturing movement on the surface of water, such as ripples. Therefore raging rapids acquired a soft, cotton-wool appearance in the final picture.

By Carleton E. Watkins ("C.E. Watkins" in ink, lower right below print), probably 1860s

15¾″ x 20¾″ on 20⅞″ x 27″ mount
From Yosemite National Park, National Park Service

58. "Section of the 'Grizzly Giant' Mariposa Grove" (Yosemite, California)

Shown is Galen Clark, the "Keeper of the Big Trees" (Naef, p. 38, fig. 49).

By Carleton E. Watkins ("C.E. Watkins" in ink, lower right below print), ca. 1866

15³⁄₁₆″ x 20⅞″ on 21″ x 27″ mount
From Yosemite National Park, National Park Service

**60. "Snow Bank in East Humboldt
Mountains"**
East Humboldt Range, Elko County,
Nevada
By Timothy H. O'Sullivan
(King survey), probably August 1868
7¾″ x 10⅝″ on 12⅜″ x 14⅝″ mount
From U.S. Geological Survey

61. Untitled
Mount Shasta (elevation 14,162 feet)
and Whitney Glacier, from Shastina,
Siskiyou County, California
By Carleton E. Watkins (King sur-
vey), 1870 (see Naef, p. 85)
8″ x 12¼″ on 12⅜″ x 14¾″ mount
From U.S. Geological Survey

**62. "Half Dome, 5000 ft. and Glacier
Point"** (Yosemite)
By Carleton E. Watkins, ca. 1866
Published by I.W. Taber, 1870s-1880s
("Taber" and "2665" imprints below
image)
8¹⁄₁₆″ x 4¹⁵⁄₁₆″ on 9⅞″ x 6⅞″ mount
From Denver Public Library

63. "Cañon del Muerte [sic] from Mummy Cave, Ariz." (in negative)

Canyon del Muerto, Canyon de Chelly National Monument, Apache County, Arizona

By John K. Hillers, for U.S. Geological Survey and/or the Bureau of Ethnology, Smithsonian Institution, ca. 1879 ("Hillers" imprint in negative)

10½″ x 13⅝″ on 16″ x 20″ mount
From U.S. Geological Survey

64. Untitled

Man on raft in Ripple Lake, White Pine Canyon, Nevada (?)

By Andrew Joseph Russell, 1867-1868 (see Naef, pl. 101, for Russell attribution).

8¾″ x 12⅛″ on 9⅛″ x 12½″ mount
From U.S. Geological Survey

**65. "Balanced Rock, Garden of the
Gods"** (in negative) (Colorado)

By William Henry Jackson ("W.H.
Jackson & Co. Phot. Denver" and
"No. 1006" in negative), after 1880

17¼″ x 21¼″ on 20″ x 24⅛″ mount
From the Colorado Historical Society

66B. "Wyoming Territory, Tertiary bluffs, near Green River City"

Bluffs north of Green River City, Wyoming Territory, now Green River, Sweetwater County, Wyoming

By Timothy H. O'Sullivan (King survey), probably 1869

8″ x 11¼″ on 12¹⁵⁄₁₆″ x 14¾″ mount

From U.S. Geological Survey

66A. "Land of the Standing Rocks"

Near the junction of the Green and Colorado Rivers, Utah

Wood engraving from Clarence E. Dutton, *Tertiary History of the Grand Cañon District.* Washington: Government Printing Office, 1882, Plate XI.

From a drawing by William Henry Holmes, based on a photograph (Dutton, p. xii), probably by John K. Hillers

5″ x 7¾″

From Smithsonian Institution Libraries

67A. "Perched Rock, Rocker Creek, Arizona"

Probably along present Rock Creek, Coconino County, Arizona

By William Bell, 1872

10⅞″ x 8″ on 14¼″ x 11⅜″ mount

From U.S. Geological Survey

67C. "Perched Rock, Rocker Creek, Arizona"

Toned lithograph by the Graphic Company, New York, from G.K. Gilbert's article in George M. Wheeler, *Report Upon Geographical and Geological Exploration and Surveys West of the One Hundreth Meridian, Vol. III. — Geology,* Washington: Government Printing Office, 1875.

Plate XI

7¾″ x 5⅞″

From Smithsonian Institution Libraries

67B. "Perched Rock, Rocker Creek, Arizona"

Stereograph by William Bell, 1872
4″ x 7″
From Denver Public Library

68A. "El Capitan, 3,300 ft., Yosemite Cal."

Attributed to Carleton E. Watkins, 1870; later published by I.W. Taber ("Taber" imprint and negative number "B411" on photograph); *cf.* Naef, plate 7

7⅞" x 5" on 9⅞" x 6⅞" mount
From Denver Public Library

68B. "El Capitan"

Wood engraving, signed "Kilburn & Cross," from William Thayer, *Marvels of the New West,* Norwich: Henry Bill Publishing Co., 1891, p.85

9⁷⁄₁₆" x 5⅞" sheet, unmounted
From Denver Public Library

69. "Hanging Rock/Echo Cañon" (Utah)

From Ferdinand V. Hayden, *Sun Pictures of Rocky Mountain Scenery,* New York: Julius Bien, 1870, Plate XVII. This was one of the earliest books on the West containing photographs, which were pasted (tipped-in) on the pages.

By Andrew Joseph Russell, ca. 1868
6" x 8" on 12" x 9⅛" mount
From Smithsonian Institution Libraries

70. Untitled
El Capitan, Yosemite, California
By Carleton E. Watkins (sign "C.E. Watkins" in ink, lower right below print), 1860s
20½″ x 16⅜″ on 25⅛″ x 20⅞″ mount
From Denver Public Library

71. "Grand Cañon of the Colorado"
(in negative)

Possibly a view in Lower Granite Gorge, Grand Canyon of the Colorado River, Mohave County, Arizona

By William Henry Jackson (for W.H. Jackson & Co., Denver), ca. 1883?

"W.H. Jackson & Co." and "No. 1068" in negative (*cf.* "No. 1069," in Naef, plate 126)

21⅛″ x 16¾″ on 21⅝″ x 17½″ mount

From U.S. Geological Survey

1068. GRAND CANON OF THE COLORADO.   W.H. JACKSON & C? DENVER.

72. "Grand Canyon Scene"
Oil on canvas by Thomas Moran,
1920 (signed and dated, lower left)
30″ x 40⅛″
From Grand Canyon National Park,
National Park Service

73. "Gunnison Butte, Green River"
Gray Canyon, Emery County, Utah
Probably by E.O. Beaman (Powell's
second Colorado River expedition),
1871
10⅛″ x 13⅝″ on 16″ x 19¾″ mount
From Denver Public Library

74. "Palace Butte Park,/Gallatin Mt's., M.T." (in negative)
Probably Hyalite (formerly Middle) Creek, upstream from present Middle Creek Reservoir; Palace Butte is west of Hyalite Creek, Gallatin County, Montana
By William Henry Jackson (Hayden survey), ca. September 15, 1872. Probably 1872 series (11″ x 14″ negatives), No. 37. See also 1872 stereoscopic series, No. 587; 1872 series (8″ x 10″ negatives), No. 476 (Jackson catalog, pp. 38, 45, 47).
10¼″ x 13¼″ on 15¾″ x 20″ mount
From Denver Public Library

76. "Canyon River??" (pencil on mount)
Inner gorge of the Grand Canyon of the Colorado River, Grand Canyon National Park, Arizona
By John K. Hillers (Powell survey), 1872 or later
17¾″ x 21⅝″ on 21⅞″ x 28″ mount
From U.S. Geological Survey

75. "Grand Cañon of the Yellowstone"
(in negative) (Wyoming)
By either William Henry Jackson (W.H. Jackson & Co., Denver) or John K. Hillers (U.S. Geological Survey), 1883 or 1885 [similar orientation in Jackson's 1871 series (8″ x 10″ negatives), No. 248 (Jackson catalog, p. 28)]
13″ x 9⅝″ on 20″ x 16″ mount
From U.S. Geological Survey

77. "Cañon of the Rio Las Animas and the Needle Mts." (in negative) (Colorado)

Probably by William Henry Jackson, 1880s, "No. 1039" in negative

16¾″ x 21⅛″ on 17⅞″ x 22⁹⁄₁₆″ mount

From the Colorado Historical Society

78. "In the Cañon of the Rio Las Animas near Rockwood"

"124" in negative, but probably same view as W.H. Jackson & Co., Denver, No. 1077, "Cañon of the Rio Animas," La Plata County, Colorado. Jackson worked for the Denver and Rio Grande Railroad in 1881 and subsequent years.

By William Henry Jackson (marked "W.H.J. & Co."), 1881 or later

10¼″ x 13½″ on 16″ x 19⅞″ mount

From Denver Public Library

▼

79. "Bridge Above Devil's Gate, U. P. ▶ Ry."

"High Bridge" of the Colorado Central Railroad over Clear Creek, Clear Creek County, Colorado. The bridge was located at the "Loop" southwest of Georgetown. At least three photographs were taken by Jackson at this site.

By William Henry Jackson, probably for W.H. Jackson & Co., Denver, April 1884

10⅛″ x 13½″ on 16″ x 19⅞″ mount

From Denver Public Library

86

81. **"Chipeta Falls, Black Cañon of the Gunnison"** (imprint in negative)
(Colorado)
Wooden crates on the flatcar probably contain photographic plates (see enlargement). "No. 1052" (imprint in negative)
By William Henry Jackson, ca. 1883
16⅞″ x 21⅛″ on 20″ x 24″ mount
From the Colorado Historical Society

80. **"Officers and Contractors, U. P. R. R."**

View near Promontory, Utah, on May 10, 1869, the day the Union Pacific and Central Pacific tracks met. Included are Grenville Mellen Dodge, Chief Engineer, UPRR (seventh from right) and Samuel Benedict Reed, Superintendent of Construction, UPRR (ninth from right). Car No. 29 is attached to Union Pacific Engine No. 119, off photograph to the right.
By Andrew Joseph Russell for the Union Pacific Railroad
9⅞″ x 11⅜″ on 10½″ x 12½″ mount
From U.S. Geological Survey

◄

82. "Trestle Work/Promontory Point, Salt Lake Valley" (Utah)

From F. V. Hayden, *Sun Pictures of Rocky Mountain Scenery,* New York: Julius Bien, 1870, Plate XXVIII

By Andrew Joseph Russell, probably 1869

6″ x 8″ on 12″ x 9⅛″ mount

From Smithsonian Institution Libraries

83A. "Rock Carved by Drifting Sand, Below Fortification Rock, Arizona"

West bank of the Colorado River, Clark County, California, probably near Ringbolt Rapids. The bottle was used for scale. Close-up views provided details of scientific and technological importance which could be used for careful study after returning from the field.

By Timothy H. O'Sullivan (Wheeler survey), 1871 series, No. 14

8″ x 10⅞″ on 11½″ x 14¼″ mount

From U.S. Geological Survey

83B. "Rock Carved by Drifting Sand, Near Mouth of Grand Wash, Utah" [sic]

The Grand Wash empties into the Colorado River just west of the Grand Canyon in Mohave County, Arizona. This heliotype, one of the numerous experimental photomechanical reproduction techniques (image reversed), by J.R. Osgood & Co., Boston, is from the O'Sullivan photograph, fig 83A. From G.K. Gilbert, "Geology . . .," in G.M. Wheeler, *Report upon Geographical and Geological Explorations and Surveys West of the One Hundredth Meridian . . . Vol. III — Geology,* Washington: Government Printing Office, 1875, Plate VIII

8⅞″ x 11⅝″

From Denver Public Library

84. "Historic Spanish Record of the Conquest/South Side of Inscription Rock, N. M. No. 3"

Spanish script carved on Inscription Rock, in present El Morro National Monument (established 1906), Valencia County, New Mexico

By Timothy H. O'Sullivan (Wheeler survey), 1873 series, No. 9

7⅝″ x 10⅞″ on 11⅝″ x 14½″ mount

From U.S. Geological Survey

85. "Lower-Pa-Ro-Gunt (Largest Cave Lake)"

Stereograph from series, *Views on Kanab Creek,* southern Utah

By John K. Hillers (Powell survey), 1871 or later. Published by J.F. Jarvis

4½″ x 7″

From Division of Photographic History, Smithsonian Institution

86A. "Tufa Mounds, Pyramid Lake, Nevada"

Anaho Island (now Anaho Island National Wildlife Refuge), Pyramid Lake, Washoe County

By Timothy H. O'Sullivan (King survey), probably 1867

7¾″ x 10⅝″ on 12⅜″ x 14¾″ mount

From U.S. Geological Survey

86B. "Tufa Bank—Anaho Island—Pyramid Lake—Nevada"

Toned lithograph by Julius Bien from O'Sullivan print, in Clarence King, *Systematic Geology*, Vol. I of *Report of the Geological Exploration of the Fortieth Parallel*, Washington: Government Printing Office, 1878, Plate XXIV

5¾″ x 8⅜″

From Smithsonian Institution Libraries

86C. "Strange Tufa"

Wood engraving, *Harper's New Monthly Magazine*, September 1869, p. 469

4½″ x 3½″

From Smithsonian Institution Libraries

88. "The old deserted ranch and station at the Three Crossings of the Sweetwater"
Valley of the Sweetwater River, Fremont County, Wyoming. Hayden survey camp in middle ground at left; note guard with rifle on watchtower at the left end of the station (see enlargement). This Overland Stage Station was abandoned after 1862 (C.S. Jackson, p.90).

By William Henry Jackson (Hayden survey), ca. August 30 or 31, 1870. From 1870 series (6½″ x 8½″ negatives) No. 97. Although the "new" No. 299 appears on this print (inscribed in negative), it is "old" No. 97 in the catalog; title from catalog, p.15. *Cf.* 1870 stereoscopic series, No. 313, p. 21. From Denver Public Library

87. "Emigrant's Grave, on the Sweetwater"

Valley of the Sweetwater River, Fremont County, Wyoming. Probably painter Sanford Robinson Gifford standing at grave or "R.T.," a soldier killed during the Indian raids in the Three Crossings area in April 1862 (C.S. Jackson, p. 91). This print forms a panorama when combined with fig. 88.

By William Henry Jackson (Hayden survey), ca. August 30 or 31, 1870 1870 series (6½″ x 8½″ negatives), No. 98. This print bears the "new" No. 300, but is actually "old" No. 98 (Jackson catalog, p. 15).

5⅝″ x 8⅛″ on 10″ x 12″ mount
From U.S. Geological Survey

89A. "Boteler's Ranch"

The name of the ranch is also spelled "Boettler" and "Bottler" (see below), but Jackson and the Hayden survey publications used "Boteler." West side of the Yellowstone Valley, near the present town of Emigrant, Park County, Montana. The man at left is unidentified, but the others, shown from left to right are: two Boteler brothers; Albert Charles Peale, Hayden survey geologist; and C. De V. Negley, Hayden survey general assistant (Bonney and Bonney, p. 226). By William Henry Jackson (Hayden survey), 1871 series (8″ x 10″ negatives), No. 203 (see Jackson catalog, p. 24)

5⅝″ x 9″ on 11″ x 14″ mount
From Denver Public Library

89B. "Bottler's Ranch/Opposite Emigrant Peak"

E. Bierstadt Albertype photomechanical reproduction of Jackson photograph (image reversed)
4¾″ x 7¾″ on 11″ x 14″ mount
From Denver Public Library

90. "Officer's quarters, Fort Ruby"

Title from Horan, p. 277. Fort (later
Camp) Ruby, White Pine County,
Nevada. Fort Ruby (1862-1869) was
abandoned after the completion of
the transcontinental railway (Frazer,
p. 94).

By Timothy H. O'Sullivan (King
survey), 1868. No. 45 on mount and in
negative

7¾″ x 10¾″ on 12½″ x 14¾″ mount
From U.S. Geological Survey

91. Untitled

Fort Ruby (same site as in fig. 90). No.
44 on mount and in negative

By Timothy H. O'Sullivan (King
survey), 1868

7¾″ x 10⅝″ on 12½″ x 14½″ mount
From U.S. Geological Survey

93

92. "Branch of the Grand Canyon of the Colorado" (pencil under print)

Probably a view down the principal east tributary (old Imp Canyon) of Tuckup Canyon, Grand Canyon National Park, Mohave County, Arizona. A Denver Public Library print bears the imprint, "Imp Cañon, Kanab Plateau, Ariz."; the exhibit print shown here, apparently made from the same negative, has the imprint in the negative, "Nan-Kun-To-Wip Valley, Utah."

Probably by John K. Hillers (Powell survey), 1872 or later

12⅞″ x 9¾″ on 20″ x 16″ mount
From U.S. Geological Survey

93A. Untitled

Yosemite Falls, California
"7810" in negative, lower left
Possibly by Carleton E. Watkins, 1860s
7¼″ x 4⅜″ on 8⁹⁄₁₆″ x 5⅜″ mount

93B. "Yosemite Falls, highest Falls in the World, 2550 feet, Cal."

Stereograph by B.W. Kilburn, copyright 1894
3½″ x 7″
Both from Denver Public Library

95

94. Untitled

South face of west and center peaks of the "Three Patriarchs," Zion National Park, Washington County, Utah

Probably by John K. Hillers (Powell survey), 1872 or later

17⅞" x 21⅝" on 21⅞" x 28" mount
From U.S. Geological Survey

95. "Mist in Kanab Canyon, Utah"

Oil on canvas by Thomas Moran, 1892

44⅜" x 38⅜"

From the National Museum of American Art, Smithsonian Institution; bequest of Mrs. Bessie B. Croffut

97B. "Boren's Gulch" (in negative)
Boren Creek, La Plata County, Colorado: mining for placer gold; note the "Long Tom" sluice box
By William Henry Jackson (Hayden survey), 1875 series (5″ x 8″ negatives), No. 272 (Jackson catalog, p. 78)
4⅜″ x 7¼″ on 11″ x 14″ mount
From U.S. Geological Survey

96. Untitled
Mining operations inside the Savage Mine, Comstock Lode, Virginia City, Storey County, Nevada. O'Sullivan used burning magnesium to provide light for photographing this scene, making it one of the first pictures to be taken with artificial light in this country. Similar photographs, however, had been made three years earlier in England.*
By Timothy H. O'Sullivan (King survey), winter 1867-1868
7¾″ x 10⅝″ on 12⅜″ x 15″ mount
From U.S. Geological Survey

97A. "Hydraulic Gold Mining,/Alder Gulch near Virginia City"
Washing bedrock, Madison County, Montana
By William Henry Jackson (Hayden survey) early July (before July 17), 1871, probably 1871 series (8″ x 10″ negatives), No. 190 (Jackson catalog, p. 23; see also Nos. 188-189, p. 23; 1872 8″ x 10″ series, No. 496, p. 46; and 1872 stereoscopic series No. 618, p. 47)
4⅞″ x 8⅞″ on 11″ x 14″ mount
From Denver Public Library

*Samson, p. 467. Similar photographs were made two years earlier (May 1865) in an English mine [see British Journal of Photography, Dec. 1876, p. 611]. In this country burning magnesium was used by Charles Waldack in July 1866 for making photographs in a cave [*The Philadelphia Photographer,* August 1866, pp. 241-2].

98A. "Gold Hill, Nevada"
Storey County, Nevada
By Timothy H. O'Sullivan (King
survey), probably 1868
7⅞″ x 10⅝″ on 11½″ x 14¹/₁₆″ mount
From U.S. Geological Survey

98B. "Gold Hill and Silver City"
Wood engraving from *Harper's New
Monthly Magazine*, September 1860, p.
466
3⅛″ x 4½″
From Smithsonian Institution
Libraries

99B. "Sandstone Walls in Cañon de Chelle, N.M./(Camp Beauty 1873)" Lithograph from O'Sullivan photograph. From George M. Wheeler, *Report upon United States Geographical Surveys West of the One Hundredth Meridian, Vol. I. — Geographical Report,* Washington: Government Printing Office, 1889, Plate X

6″ x 8½″

From Smithsonian Institution Libraries

99C. Modern photomechanical reproduction of the O'Sullivan photograph from Naef, plate 63. Photomechanical techniques highlighted the importance of photography by providing low-cost copies in printer's ink which could be mass-produced at high speed. These techniques, however, were not perfected, on a practicable, wide-scale basis until the end of the 1800s. Modern photomechanical techniques make it possible to more faithfully reproduce the tonal quality of photographs.

99A. "Sandstone Walls, Camp Beauty, Cañon de Chelle"

Stereograph, Canyon de Chelly, Canyon de Chelly National Monument, Apache County, Arizona

By Timothy H. O'Sullivan (Wheeler survey), 1873

3¹⁵⁄₁₆″ x 7″

From Division of Photographic History, Smithsonian Institution

EXPEDITION OF 1873.

1st Lieut. GEO. M. WHEELER, Corps of Engineers Commanding

100. "Cañon de Chelle/Walls of the Grand Cañon about 1200 feet in height"

Same site as fig. 99

By Timothy H. O'Sullivan, 1873 series, No. 15

11″ x 13⅞″ on 15¾″ x 19½″ mount

From Denver Public Library

101. Untitled

Shoshone Falls, from the south bank of the Snake River, Shoshone Falls State Park, Idaho

A toned lithograph of the same scene —based on a different photograph— was published in King, *Systematic Geology*, Plate XVII, as "Shoshone Falls, From Below—Idaho."

By Timothy H. O'Sullivan (King survey), 1868

12⅝″ x 14¾″ on 18″ x 24″ mount
From Denver Public Library

102. "View on Apache Lake, Sierra Blanca Range, Arizona/Two Apache Scouts in the foreground"

Probably in the White Mountains, Apache County, Arizona. The lake is probably one of the numerous small lakes to the northeast of old Fort Apache.

By Timothy H. O'Sullivan (Wheeler survey), 1873 series, No. 3

10⅞″ x 8″ on 14″ x 11⅜″ mount
From U.S. Geological Survey

103. "Aboriginal Life Among the Navajoe Indians,/Near old Fort Defiance, N.M."

The post was located at the mouth of Bonito Canyon on the west side of Black Creek, Apache County, Arizona. Fort Defiance, renamed Fort Canby in 1863-1864, became the headquarters of the Navajo Indian reservation in 1868 (Frazer, p. 8). Photographs such as this were often used for ethnological documentation. See the chromolithograph, "Aboriginal Life in the Navajo Country Near Old Fort Defiance, Ariz./1873," Wheeler, *Geographical Report*, 1889, Plate IX, a romanticized adaptation of the O'Sullivan photograph.

By Timothy H. O'Sullivan (Wheeler survey), 1873 series, No. 7A

10⅞″ x 8⅟₁₆″ on 14¼″ x 11½″ mount
From U.S. Geological Survey

104A. "Apache Braves, Arizona, 1873"
Stereograph, site unidentified
By Timothy H. O'Sullivan (Wheeler survey), 1873
$3^{15}/_{16}''$ x 7″
From Denver Public Library

104B. "The Brother Chiefs"
Stereograph, "Nu-a-gun-tits" tribal chiefs and their wives, southwestern Nevada
$4^{1}/_{2}''$ x 7″
Stereographs 104B-104F all by John K. Hillers (Powell survey), 1872 or later, are from the Division of Photographic History, Smithsonian Institution.

104C. "Kai-ar"
Stereograph, "Nu-a-gun-tits" tribe; southwestern Nevada
$4^{1}/_{2}''$ x 7″

104D. "The Watch Tower"
Stereograph, with a "U-in-ta" Indian; Wasatch Mountains, Utah
$4^{1}/_{2}''$ x 7″

104E. "Sai-ar's Home"
Stereograph, "U-in-ta" Ute Indians; Wasatch Mountains, Utah
$4^{1}/_{2}''$ x 7″

104F. "The Hunter"
Stereograph, "U-ai Nu-ints" tribe; Rio Virgen, a tributary of the Colorado River, Utah
$4^{1}/_{2}''$ x 7″

105. Untitled

Possibly at or near Camp Apache, White River, Navajo County, Arizona. Fort Apache, a U.S. Army post from 1870 to 1924, was known as "Fort Apache" from 1870 to 1871 and 1879 to 1924, but as "Camp Apache" from 1871 to 1879 (Frazer, 1965, p.3).

See O'Sullivan's "Distant View of Camp Apache, Arizona," 1873 series, No. 6

Probably by Timothy H. O'Sullivan (Wheeler survey), about 1873

8″ x 10⅞″ on 16″ x 20″ mount

From Denver Public Library

107. "Night at Valley View" (Yosemite, California)

Oil on canvas. Romanticized views such as this were sometimes criticized in the press as not being "representational" of the West.

By Albert Bierstadt, 1864

34″ x 27⅛″

From Yosemite National Park, National Park Service

106. "View from Tequa towards Moqui"
(in negative)

View from Tewa, the nothernmost of three Hopi pueblos on the southwest tip of First Mesa, looking southwest toward Second Mesa, Navajo County, Arizona. Second Mesa (on horizon at right margin) is about eight miles distant. Jackson said that the view was "south from Te-qua, showing Se-chum-e-way and Moqui. . . . They occupy nearly the entire summit of a mesa about 600 feet in height." (Jackson catalog, pp. 79-80)

By William Henry Jackson (Hayden survey), June or July 1875

From 1875 series (5″ x 8″ negatives), No. 296

4⅜″ x 7¼″ on 11″ x 14″ mount
From U.S. Geological Survey

108. "The Grotto in Eruption"

Probably a view east across the Firehole River from west of the Grotto Geyser, Upper Geyser Basin, Yellowstone National Park, Wyoming.

Probably by William Henry Jackson, either 1878 (Hayden survey), or 1883 or 1885 (for W.H. Jackson & Co., Denver). A stereograph by Jackson of the same title, 1872 series, No. 555 (Jackson catalog, p. 47), is not the same view.

16⁷⁄₁₆″ x 20⅝″ on 25″ x 30″ mount
From U.S. Geological Survey

111. "Old Faithful in Eruption" (in negative)

Probably a view from the side nearest the Firehole River, Upper Geyser Basin, Yellowstone National Park. Probably by William Henry Jackson, either 1878 (Hayden survey), or 1883 or 1885 (for W.H. Jackson & Co., Denver). See Jackson 1872 series (8″ x 10″ negatives), Nos. 440-441; and 1872 stereoscopic series, Nos. 546-547, all with same title, but not identical to this view (Jackson catalog, pp. 43, 47).

13″ x 9¾″ on 20″ x 16″ mount
From U.S. Geological Survey

110. "Grotto Geyser" (Wyoming)

Pencil on paper by Walter Trumbull, 1870

4⅛″ x 7⅜″
From Yellowstone National Park, National Park Service

109. "Yellowstone Geysers"

Wood engraving from F.V. Hayden, *Sixth Annual Report of the United States Geological Survey of the Territories ... Explorations for the Year 1872.* Washington: Government Printing Office, 1873, fig. "5" [15], facing p. 54

10½″ x 9¼″
From Smithsonian Institution Libraries

South face of the east peak of the
"Three Patriarchs," Zion National
Park, Washington County, Utah
Probably by John K. Hillers (Powell
survey), 1872 or later
17⁹⁄₁₆″ x 20¾″ on 22″ x 28″ mount
From U.S. Geological Survey

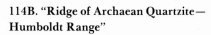

114B. "Ridge of Archaean Quartzite— Humboldt Range"
Toned photolithograph by Julius Bien from Arnold Hague and S.F. Emmons, *Descriptive Geology*, Vol. II of Clarence King, *Report of the Geological Exploration of the Fortieth Parallel,* Washington: Government Printing Office, 1877, Plate XIX
5⅞″ x 8¼″
From Smithsonian Institution Libraries

113. Untitled
Washington Column and the Royal Arches, Yosemite, California
By Carleton E. Watkins, about 1866
20½″ x 16″ on 27⅝″ x 21⅜″ mount
From Denver Public Library

114A. Untitled
Ridge near the head of "Glacier Cañon," near "Clover" [Humboldt] Peak, East Humboldt Range, Elko County, Nevada
By Timothy H. O'Sullivan (King survey), probably 1868
7⅞″ x 10¾″ on 12½″ x 14¾″ mount
From U.S. Geological Survey

115A. Untitled

Hot springs and tufa deposits in the Dixie Valley (called Osobb Valley by the King survey), Churchill County, Nevada. Title in Horan: "O'Sullivan's 'cantankerous black mules' near the edge of the mouth of a geyser in the Pahute Mountains, Nevada, 1871" (p. 262). Note darkroom outfit, upper right (see enlargement).

By Timothy H. O'Sullivan (King survey), probably 1868

7¾″ x 10⅝″ on 12¼″ x 14½″ mount
From U.S. Geological Survey

115B. "Hot Spring Tufa—Osobb Valley—Nevada"

Toned photolithograph by Julius Bien from Hague and Emmons, *Descriptive Geology,* Plate XXI, bottom
4⅛″ x 5⅝″
From Smithosonian Institution Libraries

116. Untitled

Nevada Fall, 700 ft., Yosemite,
California. Possibly by Carleton E.
Watkins, about 1866

3⅝″ x 4¾″ on 8¾″ x 10⅝″ mount
From The Library of Congress

117. Untitled

Title in Horan: "O'Sullivan's wagon and mules in the wastelands near Steamboat Springs, Nevada" (p. 164). Area surrounding Steamboat Springs, Washoe Valley, probably looking east toward the Virginia Range, Washoe County, Nevada. Includes a portion of the present Steamboat Springs geothermal area. O'Sullivan's wagon and photographic outfit shown at left.

By Timothy H. O'Sullivan (King survey), 1867

7¾″ x 10⅝″ on 12⅜″ x 14½″ mount
From U.S. Geological Survey

118. "Black Cañon, Colorado River, Looking Above from Camp 7"

View upstream from the west bank of the Colorado River above Roaring Rapids, Black Canyon, Colorado River. Standpoint in Clark County, California; the east shore of the river is in Mohave County, Arizona. O'Sullivan's boat, *Picture,* is in the center foreground.

By Timothy H. O'Sullivan (Wheeler survey), about September 22, 1871; 1871 series, No. 5

8″ x 10⅞″ on 11⅜″ x 14¼″ mount
From U.S. Geological Survey

119. Untitled
Mount Shasta and Shastina, Siskiyou
County, California; about 12 miles
from Sheep Rock
By Carleton E. Watkins (King survey), 1870
8¹⁄₁₆″ x 12¼″ on 12⁷⁄₁₆″ x 14⅝″ mount
From U.S. Geological Survey

120. "Crater of Grotto Geyser"

Probably a view east across the Firehole River from a position west of the Grotto Geyser, Upper Geyser Basin, Yellowstone National Park, Wyoming

By William Henry Jackson (Hayden survey), early August 1871. From 1871 series (8″ x 10″ negatives), No. 297 (Jackson catalog, p. 31); *cf.* 1872 series 8″ x 10″ negatives), No. 448, p. 44; 1872 series (11″ x 14″ negatives), No. 15, p. 36

E. Bierstadt Albertype photomechanical reproduction (image reversed from original print), "Plate XXI" of unidentified publication, *Hot Spring Series*

7⅝″ x 9⁹⁄₁₆″ on 11″ x 14¹⁄₁₆″ sheet
From Denver Public Library

121. "Entrance to the Teton Cañon, Aug. 27 79" (Wyoming)

Pencil on paper by Thomas Moran, 1879

10¾″ x 14¾″, irregularly cut sheet
From Grand Teton National Park, National Park Service; gift of Ruth Moran

BIBLIOGRAPHY

Abbott, Austin. "The Eye and Camera," *Harper's New Monthly Magazine,* Vol. XXXIX, No. CCXXXI (August 1869), pp. 476-482.

Alinder, James, ed., with essays by David Featherstone and Russ Anderson. *Carleton E. Watkins. Photographs of the Columbia River and Oregon.* Carmel, California: The Friends of Photography, Inc., 1979.

Bartlett, Richard A. *Great Surveys of the American West.* Norman, Oklahoma: University of Oklahoma Press, 1962.

Billington, Ray Allen. *Westward Expansion, A History of the American Frontier.* New York: Macmillan Publishing Co., Inc., Fourth Edition, 1974.

Bonney, Orrin H., and Lorraine Bonney. *Battle Drums and Geysers. The Life of Lt. Gustavus Cheyney Doane, Soldier and Explorer of the Yellowstone and Snake River Regions.* Chicago: The Swallow Press, 1970.

Boorstin, Daniel J. *The Americans: The National Experience.* New York: Vintage Books, A Division of Random House, 1965.

Bromley, Isaac H. "The Big Trees and the Yosemite. The Wonders of the West—I," *Scribner's Monthly,* Vol. 3, No. 3 (January 1872), pp. 261-276.

Bryan, George S. "Pioneers of the Great West," *The Mentor,* Volume 8, Number 1 (February 16, 1920).

Cheyenne Centennial Committee. *150 Years in Western Art.* Cheyenne, Wyoming: Pioneer Printing Stationery Co., 1967.

Current, Karen. *Photography and the Old West.* New York: Harry N. Abrams, Inc., in association with the Amon Carter Museum of Western Art, 1978. Photographs selected and printed by William R. Current.

Curti, Merle. *The Growth of American Thought.* New York; Evanston, Illinois; and London: Harper & Row, Publishers. Third edition, 1964.

Darrah, William Culp. *The World of Stereographs.* Gettysburg, Pennsylvania: W.C. Darrah, publisher, 1977.

Dellenbaugh, Frederick S. *The Romance of The Colorado River.* New York: G.P. Putnam's Sons, and London: The Knickerbocker Press, 1903.

_____. *A Canyon Voyage.* New York: G.P. Putnam's Sons, and London: The Knickerbocker Press, 1908.

Dicker, Laverne Mau. "Watkins' Photographs in the California Historical Society Library," *California History,* Vol. LVII, No. 3 (Fall 1978), pp. 266-270.

Fairbanks, Jonathan L. Museum of Fine Arts, Boston. *Frontier America: The Far West.* Boston: The Leether Press, 1975.

Fern, Thomas S. *The Drawings and Watercolors of Thomas Moran (1837-1926).* Notre Dame, Indiana: The Art Gallery, University of Notre Dame, 1976.

Fowler, Don D.,ed. *Photographed All the Best Scenery. Jack Hiller's Diary of the Powell Expeditions, 1871-1875.* Salt Lake City, Utah: University of Utah Press, 1972.

Frazer, Robert W. *Forts of the West, Military Forts and Presidios and Posts Commonly Called Forts West of the Mississippi River to 1898.* Norman, Oklahoma: University of Oklahoma Press, 1965.

Frémont, Brevet Captain J[ohn] C[harles]. *Report of The Exploring Expedition to The Rocky Mountains, in the Year 1842 and to Oregon and North California in the years 1843-'44.* Washington, D.C.: Gales and Seaton, Printers, 1845.

Goetzmann, William H. *William H. Holmes Panoramic Art.* Fort Worth, Texas: Amon Carter Museum of Western Art, 1977.

_____. *Exploration and Empire: The Explorer and the Scientist in the Winning of the American West.* New York: Alfred A. Knopf, 1966.

Grenbeaux, Pauline. "Before Yosemite Art Gallery: Watkins' Early Career," *California History,* Vol. LVII, No. 3 (Fall 1978), pp. 220-241.

Hague, Arnold, and S.F. Emmons. *Descriptive Geology.* Washington, D.C.: U.S. Government Printing Office, 1877. Vol. II of Clarence King, *Report of the Geological Exploration of the Fortieth Parallel.*

Hamerton, Philip Gilbert. *Painter's Camp.* Boston: Roberts Brothers, 1867.

Hayden, F[erdinand] V[andeveer]. "More about the Yellowstone. The Wonders of the West—II," *Scribner's Monthly,* Vol. 3, No. 4 (February 1872), pp. 388-396.

_____. *Geological and Geographical Atlas of Colorado and Portions of Adjacent Territory.* Department of the Interior. United States Geological and Geographical Surveys of the Territories, 1877. Julius Bien, lith.

_____. *Sixth Annual Report of the United States Geological Survey of the Territories... Explorations for the Year 1872.* Washington, D.C.: U.S. Government Printing Office, 1873.

_____. *Sun Pictures of Rocky Mountain Scenery, with a Description of the Geographical and Geological Features, and Some Account of the Resources of the Great West; Containing Thirty Photographic Views Along the Line of the Pacific Rail Road, from Omaha to Sacramento.* New York: Julius Bien, 1870.

_____. *Twelfth Annual Report of the United States Geological Survey of the Territories... Explorations for the Year 1878.* Washington, D.C.: U.S. Government Printing Office, 1883.

Hoobler, Dorothy and Thomas. *Photographing The Frontier.* Toronto: Academic Press Canada Limited, 1980.

Horan, James D. *Timothy O'Sullivan: America's Forgotten Photographer.* Garden City, New York: Doubleday, 1966.

Huth, Hans. *Nature and the American. Three Centuries of Changing Attitudes.* Berkeley and Los Angeles, California: University of California Press, 1957.

Ives, Lieutenant Joseph C[hristmas]. *U.S. Engineer Dept. Report Upon the Colorado River of the West. Under the Direction of the Office of Explorations and Surveys. A.A. Humphreys, Captain Topographical Engineers, in Charge.* Washington, D.C.: U.S. Government Printing Office, 1861.

Jackson, Clarence S. *Picture Maker of the Old West, William H. Jackson.* New York and London: Charles Scribner's Sons, Ltd.

Jackson, William Henry. *The Diaries of William Henry Jackson, Frontier Photographer.* Ann W. and Leroy R. Hafen, eds. Glendale, California: The Arthur H. Clark Company, 1959.

_____. *Descriptive Catalogue of the Photographs of the United States Geological Survey of the Territories, for the Years 1869 to 1875, Inclusive.* Second Edition. Department of the Interior, United States Geological Survey of the Territories, F.V. Hayden, U.S. Geologist-in-Charge. Miscellaneous Publications —No. 5. Washington, D.C.: U.S. Government Printing Office, 1875. Available in a fascimile reprint published by Raymond Dworczyk, The Q Press, Milwaukee, Wis., 1978.

_____. *Time Exposure. The Autobiography of William Henry Jackson.* New York: G.P. Putnam's Sons, 1940.

_____. In collaboration with Howard R. Driggs. *The Pioneer Photographer. Rocky Mountain Adventures with a Camera.* Pioneer Life Series. Yonkers-on-Hudson, New York: World Book Company, 1929.

Jarves, James Jackson. *Art Thoughts.* New York and London: Garland Publishing, Inc., 1976.

Johnston, J.E., and others. *Reports of the Secretary of War with Reconnaissances of Routes from San Antonio to El Paso... July 24, 1850.* Washington, D.C.: U.S. Government Printing Office, 1850.

King, Clarence. *Mountaineering in the Sierra Nevada.* Boston: James R. Osgood and Company, 1872. Reprinted 1935 by W.W. Norton & Company, Inc., New York.

_____. *Report of the Geological Exploration of the Fortieth Parallel. Vol. I, Systematic Geology.* Washington, D.C.: U.S. Government Printing Office, 1878.

Mangan, Terry Wm. *Colorado On Glass. Colorado's First Half Century As Seen by the Camera.* Denver, Colorado: Sundance Limited, 1975.

Morton, Rogers C.B. "National Parks' Centennial Year," in *National Parks and the American Landscape.* Washington, D.C.: The Smithsonian Institution Press, 1972.

Naef, Weston, in collaboration with James N. Wood. *Era of Exploration: The Rise of Landscape Photography in the American West, 1860-1885.* Buffalo, New York: Albright-Knox Art Gallery, and New York: The Metropolitan Museum of Art, 1975.

Newhall, Beaumont. *The History of Photography from 1839 to the Present Day.* New York: The Museum of Modern Art, 1949.

Ostroff, Eugene. *Photographing the Frontier.* Washington, D.C.: Smithsonian Institution Press, 1976.

Palmquist, Peter E. "California's Peripatetic Photographer, Charles Leander Weed," *California History,* Vol. LVIII, No. 3 (Fall 1979), pp. 194-219.

_____. "Watkins—The Photographer as Publisher," *California History,* Vol. LVII, No. 3 (Fall 1978), pp. 252-257.

Preuss, Charles. *Exploring With Frémont. The Private Diaries of Charles Preuss, Cartographer for John C. Frémont on His First, Second, and Fourth Expeditions to the Far West.* Translated and edited by Erwin G. and Elizabeth K. Gudde. Norman, Oklahoma: University of Oklahoma Press, 1958.

Richards, T. Addison. "The Arts of Design in America, from 1780 to the Present Time," *Eighty Years' Progress of the United States: A Family Record of American Industry, Energy and Enterprise...* Vol. II, Hartford, Connecticut: L. Stebbins, 1867, pp. 317-336.

Rudisill, Richard. "Watkins and the Historical Record," *California History,* Vol. LVII, No. 3. (Fall 1978), pp. 216-219.

Samuels, Peggy and Harold. *The Illustrated Biographical Encyclopedia of Artists of the American West.* Garden City, New York: Doubleday & Company, Inc., 1976.

Savage, Henry Jr. *Discovering America 1700-1875.* New York: Harper & Row Publishers, 1979.

Sexton, Nanette. "Watkins' style and Technique in the Early Photographs," *California History,* Vol. LVII, No. 3 (Fall 1978), pp. 242-251.

Sheldon, G.W. *American Painters: With One Hundred and Four Examples of Their Work Engraved on Wood.* New York: D. Appleton and Company, 1881.

Sobieszek, Robert. "Alexander Gardner's Photographs Along the 35th Parallel," *Image,* Vol. 14, No. 3 (June 1971), pp. 6-8.

Taft, Robert. "A Photographic History of Early Kansas," *The Kansas Historical Quarterly,* Vol. III, No. 1 (February 1934), pp. 3-14.

_____. *Photography and the American Scene. A Social History, 1839-1889.* New York: The Macmillan Company, 1938. Reprinted Dover Publications, 1964.

Thayer, William Makepeace. *Marvels of the New West.* Norwich, Connecticut: Henry Bill Pub. Co., 1891.

Tilden, Freeman. *Following the Frontier with F. Jay Haynes, Pioneer Photographer of the Old West.* New York: Alfred A. Knopf, 1964.

Wheeler, George M. *Report upon United States Geographical Surveys West of the One Hundredth Meridian. Vol. I — Geographical Report.* Washington, D.C.: U.S. Government Printing Office, 1889.

_____. *Report upon United States Geographical and Geological Exploration and Surveys West of the One Hundredth Meridian . . . Vol. III, Geology.* Washington, D.C.: U.S. Government Printing Office, 1875.

_____. *Photographs Showing Landscapes, Geological and Other Features, of Portions in the Western Territory of the United States, Obtained in Connection with the Geographical and Geological Explorations West of the 100th Meridian Seasons of 1871, 1872, and 1873.* Washington, D.C.: U.S. Government Printing Office, 1875(?).

_____. *Progress-Report upon Geographical and Geological Explorations and Surveys, West of the One Hundredth Meridian, 1872.* Washington, D.C.: U.S. Government Printing Office, 1874.

Wood, Ruth Kedzie. "The Lewis and Clark Expedition," *The Mentor,* Volume 7, Number 6, May 1, 1919.